W9-DBZ-998

THE ART of BAKING with NATURAL YEAST

BREADS, PANCAKES, WAFFLES, CINNAMON ROLLS & MUFFINS

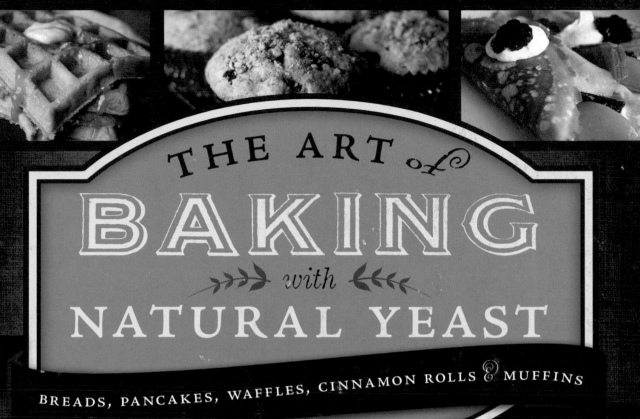

THE ART of BAKING

with

NATURAL YEAST

BREADS, PANCAKES, WAFFLES, CINNAMON ROLLS & MUFFINS

CALEB WARNOCK & MELISSA RICHARDSON

FRONT TABLE BOOKS
AN IMPRINT OF CEDAR FORT, INC.
SPRINGVILLE, UTAH

ISBN 13: 978-1-4621-1048-3

Published by Front Table Books, an imprint of Cedar Fort, Inc.
2373 W. 700 S., Springville, UT, 84663

Distributed by Cedar Fort, Inc., www.cedarfort.com

LIBRARY OF CONGRESS CATALOGING-IN-PUBLICATION DATA

    Warnock, Caleb (Caleb J.), 1973- author.
    Bread, naturally : a modern guide to the health benefits of an ancient tradition /
    Caleb Warnock and Melissa Richardson.
       pages cm
    ISBN 978-1-4621-1048-3
    1. Bread. 2. Cooking (Bread) I. Richardson, Melissa, author. II. Title.
    TX769.W33 2012
    641.81'5--dc23
                    2012002122

Cover and book design by Angela D. Olsen
Edited by Melissa Caldwell
Cover design © 2012 by Lyle Mortimer

Printed in China

10   9   8   7   6   5   4   3   2   1

Printed on acid-free paper

DEDICATIONS

MY FIRST GRATITUDE goes to my coauthor, Melissa Richardson, for hundreds of hours of baking and writing to make this book possible. I'm grateful for the day she brought that first loaf of bread to my writing class. Thanks also to Melissa's husband and kids for welcoming me into their home.

Thank you to Ginger Anderson Livingston of Ginger Snaps Photography for taking the mouthwatering photos in this book. Huge thanks to Loraine Scott, who let us borrow her gorgeous kitchen for a messy four-hour photo shoot with very little notice. You are a true friend.

Particular thanks to my writing friends and students for their strong encouragement—especially to Elaine Hume, Loraine Scott, Julie Peterson, Stacy "Magda" Kupiec, Melody Johnson, Betsy Schow, Tanya Hanamaikai, Scott Livingston, Matt and Brooklyn Evans, Laura Dene Low, Ginger Churchill, Eric James Stone, Chrisy Ross, Jenifer Lee, Cindy Bechtold, Janiel Miller, Maegan Langer, Steph Lineback, and Cally Nielson.

Thanks to the hundreds of people who have taken natural yeast baking classes from me and Melissa, and have encouraged and sometimes even demanded that we write this book. And to my last living grandparent, "Billie" Nielson—I love you, Grandma. Having you visit my garden and feed my chickens with Xander was one of my best days.

This book is dedicated to my wife, Charmayne Gubler Warnock. Everything in my life has been better since we joined hands inside Plato's Cave.

—CALEB

I WOULD LIKE TO THANK my wonderful husband, Troy, for all his support in my bread adventures and for always being willing to eat the results, even when an experiment didn't quite make the cut. Thanks to my beautiful children, who supported me every day of this process with helping hands, willing appetites, and big slobbery kisses. Thanks to my parents, Laurie and Daniel Seron; in-laws Carolyn Moss and J and Joanna Richardson; sister, Sarah Seron; and dear friends for showing their unconditional support through babysitting—I never would have survived without you! And to my siblings, Daniel, Joseph, James, Sarah, and Michael Seron, for supporting me, because that's what family does.

This book never would have been written without my coauthor Caleb Warnock. Before his invitation to attempt this project, I never in my wildest dreams would have thought of being published. Thank you, Caleb, for forcing me to dream big!

Thanks to Nancy Brook for all her natural yeast wisdom and knowledge. To Ginger Livingston, our photographer, a million thanks for her flexibility, cheerfulness, and willingness to get her hands dirty. Thanks to my Smashing writers group and to all my friends in the Wednesday writers class for permitting me to bring both bread and recipes to meetings for critiques.

I owe a big thank-you to all the attendees of our yeast classes for their contributions, but especially to Julie Peterson, Janet Blackwelder, and Mindy Carruth for attending nearly every class I have ever taught. To Loraine Scott for the use of her gorgeous kitchen on our first day of shooting. Most of all, thanks to my Father in Heaven for the ability to write this book, and to you, for letting me bring my passion into your kitchen!

—MELISSA

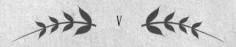

V

VI

CONTENTS

A Bread Geek Is Born

I STARTED BAKING BREAD to shave pennies off my food budget. I don't know if it really worked, but it was great breezing past the bread aisle of the grocery store every week. I felt so domestic. Unfortunately, this illusion shattered when my neighbor brought over a neatly wrapped honey whole wheat loaf that she had not only baked, but also ground her own flour for. In my whole life I had never heard of someone grinding their own flour. The bread in my hand taunted me with levels of domesticity I had never known existed. All I knew was that I had to learn to bake like Krista Wells.

I READ BOOKS AND scalped recipes to learn the art of baking with whole wheat. I baked and experimented, and my husband begged me to go back to my pre-Krista white loaves. Then one day, everything came together. My loaves were perfect and beautiful. I had arrived. Not only was I pinching pennies, I was doing so in a way that was healthier for my small family.

THAT'S WHEN I came across a news snippet claiming that people who ate whole wheat bread were more prone to digestive illnesses like celiac disease. The reporter listed multiple negative side effects found in people consuming a 100 percent whole wheat diet, stating that further investigation was underway. I couldn't believe it. People across the globe have been eating whole wheat since Eve whipped up the first loaf (Genesis 3:19), so why did it take all these thousands of years to start killing us? The logic didn't make sense.

I ALSO COULD NOT bring myself to believe that white bread was the answer to solving 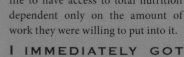 these problems, as the report had implied. Why would a God in heaven who loves his children create and advertise a "staff of life" available in non-lethal form only to the few people in the world with access to a corner grocery store? The God I know would provide a way for all human life to have access to total nutrition dependent only on the amount of work they were willing to put into it.

I IMMEDIATELY GOT to work researching in defense of my beloved whole wheat loaves. But the more I read, the guiltier my loaves looked. Whole wheat products were "proven" to cause inflammation, to aggravate our digestive systems, to "steal" vitamins and minerals from us, or to cause one of many diseases or disorders.

NOT ONLY DID IT APPEAR that my wholesome whole wheat loaves were holding out on me, I was increasing the risk my family would develop one of these problems by feeding the bread to them. Still, all that information didn't settle my gut feeling (no pun intended) that something was wrong with this mass-labeling of whole wheat bread. It didn't make sense that the growing epidemic of intestinal disease was occurring after wheat bread was nearly a thing of the past. The answer turned out to be not in the wheat, but in the yeast.

NOT TOO LONG AGO, people made bread that used natural yeast. The process required a longer rising period and more planning. Without commercial yeast, they had no choice. What they didn't know was that these longer rise (also known as a pre-ferment, sponge, or pre-digestion) periods were protecting them from the harmful enzymes causing all the trouble mentioned in the research I had found. Natural yeasts created a soil-like acidity in dough that broke down gluten to safe levels and turned nutrient-leeching phytic acid into a cancer-fighting anti-oxidant. Maximum nutrition without the nasty side effects, just as God intended.

WHAT HAD SEEMED like a time-consuming chore was really the key to whole grain health. So what happened? Food had gone industrial, commercial, and synthetic in the span of a few short decades. Quick-rise yeasts cut bread making into a couple of hours. Commercial and domestic bakers could make more bread in less time than ever before in history. Amazing.

WHAT THE VAST MAJORITY of America didn't realize then (and still doesn't realize now) is that this modern method of bread making bypasses a process designed and used over thousands of years to keep us healthy and thriving.

I HAD FOUND THE KEY to whole wheat nutrition in what had felt like a "holy grail" expedition, and my challenge now was to bring it home to my own kitchen. After years of studying and experimenting with various techniques and learning from dozens of professionals from all over the globe (the Internet is an amazing thing), I found a method that was more accommodating to my hectic lifestyle than any other I had found in all my searching.

It made such a difference in my ability to bake with natural yeast for my family that I started experimenting with ways to use natural yeast in all my baking. The results were fantastic.

I WAS SO EXCITED about sharing the results of my hard work that I started bringing samples to my weekly writing class. Not only did everyone love the bread, but I found it was a lot harder for my teacher to criticize my writing when his mouth was stuffed full of garlic rosemary sourdough. After a few months of weekly samples, my teacher (Caleb Warnock) asked me to co-author a naturally yeasted bread book with him. Two years later, we have this cookbook, full of everything I have learned and the happy results of thousands more experiments in my own home kitchen.

THERE IS STILL so much to learn, and there are so many more recipes to create, but I am excited to have this chance to share with you everything I have learned so far. You may never go to the "Bread Geek" extremes that I have, but you will find that as you learn this art and provide nutrition for the ones you love, you will enjoy the dietary self-reliance you have brought into your home. Good luck, and have fun!

LUCKY FOR US, it's not too late to learn the skills perfected by our ancestors. Yes, it takes more time than a jog to the corner grocery, but I'd much rather spend that time in my kitchen surrounded by family than in the doctor's office, wouldn't you? And so, my quest to master the art of natural yeast began.

1
NATURAL YEAST

What Is Natural Yeast?

MOST PEOPLE don't know that grocery store yeast is not a naturally occurring substance. Since 1984, the vast majority of yeast has been man-made and laboratory created. This means that for the first time in 6,000 years, humans are eating bread that is not made with natural yeast. Some people are now beginning to ask if this synthetic yeast is making us sick.

COMMERCIAL "INSTANT" YEAST was created to be fast, and is called quick or fast-rise yeast. In fact, the quick yeast produced for store-bought brands is so foreign to our digestive systems that some people develop allergies to the yeast itself. Sure, it frees up the schedule a bit. But when you consider that every culture across the globe has been using the same system for thousands of years, you have to wonder whether throwing that tried and true system out the window is considered progress.

DON'T GET US WRONG. We are no enemy of commercial yeast. In today's frenzied world, anything that can help parents provide home-baked goodness for their loved ones is a good thing. You've heard the saying "Good, better, best, never let it rest," meaning that there is always room for personal improvement. We're going to apply that saying to bread baking:

GOOD = Buying whole wheat bread from the store.

BETTER = Making your own whole wheat bread with instant yeast.

BEST = Making your own whole wheat bread with *natural* yeast.

NATURAL YEAST has several health benefits that you can't get from instant yeast:

1. Natural yeast breaks down harmful enzymes in grains.

2. Natural yeast takes the nutrition in grains—the vitamins and minerals our bodies crave—and makes them easily available for digestion.

3. Natural yeast converts dough into a digestible food source that will not spike your body's defenses. It predigests sugars for diabetics, breaks down gluten for the intolerant, and turns calcium-leaching phytic acid into a cancer-fighting antioxidant.

LET'S TAKE A CLOSER LOOK at how this system works.

3

A Natural History of Yeast, and Why It Matters

WILD, NATURAL YEAST is everywhere—in the air you breathe, on the bark of trees, on leaves. Have you ever seen the white film on backyard grapes? That's wild yeast. The same film can be found on juniper berries. For centuries, both berries have been used as a natural "start" for bread yeast.

Yeast is a single-celled fungus, and it's the first domesticated living creature in history. Modern science has identified more than 1,000 different varieties of wild yeast. These organisms are so small that hundreds of millions, if not billions, fit into a single teaspoon.

Once you have learned to maintain a natural yeast start in your own home, you will never have to buy commercial yeast again.

But not all yeast varieties are the same. For example, the kind of yeast used to make beer is not the same kind of yeast used to make bread. Different natural yeasts have different flavors—some are strongly sour, some are mildly sour, and some are not sour at all. Some are better at raising bread than others. This is why the best strains of natural yeast have been passed down through generations and communities.

Until the nineteenth century, homemade yeast was the only kind there was. In 1857, Louis Pasteur discovered that living organisms—yeasts—were responsible for fermentation. Yeast was already an important business, even though no one had understood exactly how it worked. Founded in 1853 and based in France, Société Industrielle Lesaffre is the world's leading producer of yeast and sells commercial yeast in more than 180 countries today. In the United States, it is marketed as Red Star yeast. The company was created when two cousins, Louis Lesaffre-Roussel and Louis Bonduelle Dalle, started a distillery producing ethanol from juniper berries and grain. In the early 1870s, an industrial way to extract specific kinds of yeast was invented. In 1873, Lesaffre built the first plant for producing fresh yeast.[1]

Meanwhile, in the United States, competition was brewing. The Fleischmann brothers built a yeast plant in Cincinnati, Ohio, and "patented a compressed yeast cake that revolutionized home and commercial baking." In 1876, the Fleischmanns took their invention to Philadelphia's Centennial Exposition, which drew ten million visitors. "By the end of the Exposition, America had discovered Compressed Yeast Cake and Fleischmann's Yeast had become a household word."

When America entered World War II, the company laboratories developed Active Dry Yeast® for the military, which did not require refrigeration. In 1984, "Fleischmann's did it again with RapidRise™ yeast. This highly active, finer grain of dry yeast raises dough as much as 50 percent faster than regular active dry yeast. No wonder RapidRise is the yeast of choice for busy bakers today."[2]

The 1980s also saw another trend—the beginning of a continuing spike in celiac disease, gluten intolerance, acid-reflux disease, diabetes, and wheat allergies. There is evidence that using natural yeast can help combat these problems. We do know some things for sure.

One woman in Pleasant Grove, Utah, recently told us that her husband, who is severely diabetic, was able to eat bread for the first time in years with no glycemic spike when she began making bread for him with a start of natural yeast we gave her. She first tested him on natural yeast waffles, and now he is able to eat bread on a regular basis. Several people with celiac disease have tried bread made with natural yeast and told us they had no reaction to it. Caleb Warnock, coauthor of this cookbook, had been taking prescription medication for severe acid-reflux disease for twelve years until he stopped eating white bread and started eating only 100 percent whole wheat bread made with natural yeast. He has not had a single day of heartburn since. He also lost twenty pounds.

The slow-rising process of natural yeast has many critically important health benefits. Here is what science can prove:

1. Natural yeast slows digestion to help you feel full longer, making it a natural way to eat less.

2. The organic acids produced during natural yeast fermentation lower the glycemic index of bread.[3]

3. Best of all, natural yeast lowers the body's glycemic response to all carbohydrates. An intriguing 2009 study showed that not only did natural yeast bread lower the glycemic response better than whole wheat bread made with commercial yeast, but the body's glycemic response also remained lower when eating a meal hours later. No other kind of bread produced the same result.[4]

A large, randomized clinical trial has shown that brewer's yeast—long used as a health supplement—combined with selenium potentially lowers the risk of several cancers compared to a placebo.

1. A yeast-based product has been shown in clinical trials to reduce the incidence of cold and flu. Another yeast-based product has been shown to simultaneously boost the immune system and improve bone health.

2. A University of Michigan study showed that a once-a-day supplement of a yeast-derived compound called EpiCor significantly reduced seasonal allergy symptoms, including nasal congestion, runny nose, and watery eyes.[5]

3. Natural yeast bread counteracts "the deleterious effects of whole wheat on iron absorption, whereas sourdough bread making enhanced iron absorption" and "is a better source of available minerals, especially magnesium, iron, and zinc."[6]

4. The lactic acid and natural salts in sourdough bread slow down digestion, which means you feel full longer.[7]

5. Unwanted food-borne fungi are no match for the lactic acid produced by natural yeast, which has been shown to inhibit the growth of certain bacteria and mold. And sourdough bread has long been known to have a longer shelf life.[8]

6. Natural yeast is a time-tested source of the beneficial bacteria that we all need to get the most nutrition and essential minerals from the digestion process. "In the normal scheme of things, we'd never have to think twice about replenishing the bacteria that allow us to digest food," said Sandor Ellix Katz, author of *Wild Fermentation: The Flavor, Nutrition, and Craft of Live-Culture Foods*, in a newspaper interview. Katz called antibiotics "chlorinated water," and antibacterial soap "factors in our contemporary lives that I'd group together as a 'war on bacteria.' . . . If we fail to replenish [good bacteria], we won't effectively get nutrients out of the food we're eating."[9]

Notes

1. Data from the International Directory of Company Histories
2. Breadworld.com.
3. 2004, Emerging Food Research and Development Report
4. 2009, University of Guelph, Ontario
5. Biotech Business Week
6. Nutrition, 2003
7. *Time* magazine, March 1997
8. *Life Science Weekly*
9. Sandor Ellix Katz, *Wild Fermentation: The Flavor, Nutrition, and Craft of Live-Culture Foods*

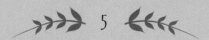

ANATOMY OF WHEAT

WHEAT IS A SEED

Wheat grains were designed to pass through the digestive tracts of grazing animals and then be "planted" on the other end in its own private fertilizer patty. Wheat can survive digestion or be stored for years without losing its ability to become a plant. How does it do this?

Wheat kernels, known as wheat berries, are plant starter kits. They contain the oils, nutrients, simple sugars, and fiber needed to grow wheat grass.

Inside the wheat berry, nutrients such as calcium, zinc, iron, magnesium, and phosphate are chained and guarded like prisoners in a fortress by a little guy called phytic acid. His job is to hold on to every nutrient until an enzyme called phytase, the lookout in the watchtower, gives him the all clear.

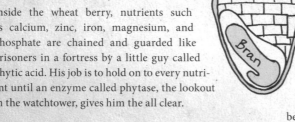

When wheat is ground into flour, it blasts some of those chains and frees a few nutrients. While the wheat flour moves through our digestive tract, phytic acid panics and runs around snatching up all nutrients that fit the description of the ones he was holding on to. Remember, his job is to make sure that none of those nutrients are digested. He does such a good job that he snatches up nutrients from other foods we've been eating. We never even realize we've been "robbed."

So how do we get phytic acid to "stand down" and release the nutrients? We have to deal with phytase, the guy in the watchtower. We use natural yeast to "trick" phytase into thinking the seed has been planted and it's time for the nutrients to go to work. This is because natural yeast starters are acidic, low in pH, and moist—just like soil.

When we work our starter into a dough, phytase recognizes the change in environment and gives the all clear for the nutrients to be released. On average, this process takes at least six hours, as the starter reproduces and spreads throughout the dough, neutralizing the phytic acid as it goes.

But here's the best part: once phytic acid has completed his assignment, he gets a new one. He runs around with his empty chains and snatches up cancer-causing free-radicals. So the good stuff gets to us, and the bad stuff gets carted off.

THE STAFF OF LIFE

JAMES SIMMONS, author of *Original Fast Foods* and food guru extraordinaire, wrote a blog post entitled "Bread, the Staff of Life." He proposed that unlike popular interpretation of that motto, it does not mean that bread is the star of the dietary show. It means that bread is a nutritional aid and should be relied upon only as much as a staff is for walking.

Using Mr. Simmons's metaphor to analyze our own society, it would seem that what used to be a staff has now become a crutch.

Have we crippled ourselves with the overuse of grains? A simple test will tell. Try limiting your daily intake of grains to the actual daily recommended intake. For most people aged nine to fifty, the recommendation is six one-ounce servings. In general, one slice of bread, one cup of ready-to-eat cereal, or a half cup of cooked rice, cooked pasta, or cooked cereal can be considered as a one ounce equivalent from the grains group.

How many adjustments do you have to make to the way you eat? If you can go at least a week without having to re-invent breakfast, lunch, and dinner as your family knows it, then you're probably in the clear. If not, take one meal at a time and explore your options for eliminating excessive grains.

This cookbook offers a large variety of recipes, not so you'll eat bread at all hours of the day, but so you'll have plenty of options for how to eat the grains you're allotted for each day.

Here's one example of how I have attempted bread-balance in my own family's diet:

BREAKFAST	CREPES with fresh fruit and yogurt or with eggs, spinach, and mushrooms
LUNCH	FLATBREAD stuffed with tomatoes, avocados, lettuce, and turkey
DINNER	BUTTERED slice of toast or roll with a large salad and hearty vegetable soup or stew

If you were counting, you would notice that (depending on the number of crepes and rolls consumed), you are consuming only around four of your six allotted ounces of whole grains. This gives you flexibility in the area of snacks and accompaniments to your meals. By eating moderate portions, you free up intake for a cup of rice with dinner, a snack of popcorn, or some granola when you get the munchies.

Let your deliciously healthy bread be the perfect complement to the vegetables and protein that make up the bulk of your meal. When we learn to keep balance in our diet, we find that we no longer need a crutch to hobble on our way. We become strong, healthy, and nutritionally independent.

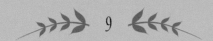

WHEAT FLOUR BENEFITS

HERE ARE A FEW REASONS

to stick with whole wheat flour:

1. Refined flour, which has had nearly all its fiber removed and thus requires little chewing, has led to an increase in gum disease, according to many experts.

2. The refining process takes away half of wheat's natural B vitamins.

3. It removes 90 percent of vitamin E.

4. Without the natural fiber that would have slowed digestion, starch is more easily digested by the body, leading to rapid jumps in glucose and insulin levels. Once inside the body, starch is metabolized like sugar. "Not only does this quick rise and fall trigger overeating through a sense of hunger, eventually a diet based on refined carbohydrates leads to greater risk for obesity, diabetes, and heart disease," according to Harvard Public Health Review 2000.

Healthy eating means whole grains. Harvard University studies, among others, show startling benefits, which we will paraphrase here:

1. Eating whole grains substantially lowers total cholesterol, bad cholesterol, triglycerides, and insulin levels.

2. Women who ate 2 to 3 daily servings of whole grains were 30 percent less likely to have a heart attack or die from heart disease than women who ate less than 1 serving per week.

3. Heart attack, stroke, or heart bypass surgery was 21 percent less likely in people who ate 2.5 or more servings of whole grains a day.

4. An eighteen-year study of 160,000 women showed that those who averaged 2 to 3 servings of whole grains a day were 30 percent less likely to have developed type 2 diabetes than those who rarely ate whole grains.

5. Women who had 2 or more servings of whole grains a day were 30 percent less likely to have died from inflammation-related conditions.

How do whole grains do all this? The answer is clear-cut, according to Harvard research:

1. Fiber slows the breakdown of starches into glucose.

2. Soluble fiber lowers cholesterol.

3. Insoluble fiber helps digestion.

4. Fiber may "help prevent the formation of small blood clots that can trigger heart attacks or strokes."

5. Antioxidants may prevent cholesterol-clogged arteries.

6. Plant estrogens in whole grains may protect against some cancers, along with magnesium, selenium, copper, and manganese, which are found naturally in whole grains. Heart disease and diabetes may also be prevented by these minerals.

Anatomy of a Starter

As we mentioned earlier, once you have learned to maintain a natural yeast start in your own home, you will never have to buy commercial yeast again. You can multiply your yeast and give it away to friends and family. You can freeze it, dry it, keep it in the fridge, or on the counter. Nothing could be simpler.

In the following chapter we'll go over how to get or make your own starter, but for now let's learn the basics. Natural yeast starter is a wet doughy mix, not a powder. It is often stored in glass canning jars. In a starter, flour and water form the "apartment complex" that houses an entire ecosystem of beneficial organisms. This ecosystem is made up of two primary organisms: lactobacilli and wild yeasts. Both need food, water, air, and shelter to survive, just like us. In fact, it is partially from us that these organisms find their way into our starters.

Wild yeast and lactobacilli exist on everything in, on, and around us. They are on our hair, our skin, even our breath. They are part of our digestive system and boost digestive health when consumed (think yogurt). In nature, they thrive on the skins of fruits and grains. Wild yeasts are captured by adding organic grapes,

apples, rye, wheat, or even juniper berries with a little water and flour, and allowing the mixture to ferment and grow. The white film that grows on these foods is, in fact, wild yeast.

The mixture of flour and water is a feeding ground for this little ecosystem. Lactobacilli and wild yeasts feed on the simple sugars in the flour and break down harsh counterparts like gluten. As they feed, they release carbon dioxide, creating bubbles of gas in the starter. The carbon dioxide is what allows natural yeast to raise bread. Another byproduct of their feeding is a brownish liquid that collects on the surface, made up of ethanol and acetic acid. The liquid is harmless and can be poured off.

Here is a basic outline of the part each one plays in a starter:

LACTOBACILLI:

1. Converts sugar to lactic acid

2. Neutralize phytic acid

3. Create ethanol (alcohol), lactic acid, and small amounts of CO_2

4. Secretes a sort of antibiotic that kills bad bacteria

5. Outnumber yeasts 100:1

WILD YEASTS:

1. Converts simple sugars and starches into ethanol (alcohol) and acetic acid (vinegar)

2. Produce CO_2 that raises the bread

3. Give off ethanol (alcohol), acetic acid (vinegar), and enough CO_2 to raise bread

WHAT DO THEY DO?

- **ETHANOL & ACETIC ACID:** create sour taste

- **LACTIC ACID:** Natural antibiotic against bad organisms

- **CARBON DIOXIDE:** Makes bubbles and raises bread

Ethanol
Acetic Acid

CO_2

wild yeasts

Lactobacilli

"You Mean My Bread Is ALIVE?"

IT'S NOT OFTEN that natural yeast skeptics can catch me without a witty response to their critical questions, but it happens from time to time. In one such class, I was explaining the beauty of the lactobacilli human circle of love when a particularly doubtful raw-foodist said, "Yeah, except then you bake your little 'friends' and everything dies and your bread is dead. How does that help you?" I had no response. None whatsoever. So I told the truth. I told her I didn't know, got her email, and said I'd get back to her on it. Then I carried on with the class, trying to hide my ruffled feathers.

HER QUESTION really bothered me. Sure the organisms did a lot of great work on the wheat before they "died," but then how do they continue to work as probiotics in our digestive system like I had been taught they did?

THE ANSWER CAME a few days later when I discovered a two-week old loaf of bread hidden in the back of the cupboard. I had done a lot of baking, and that loaf had been shoved to the back

and passed over. It was still perfectly good, no mold or other signs of going bad. I pulled it out, cut a slice, buttered it, and started to nibble. Guess what? The taste of the bread had changed. It now tasted exactly the way my starter tastes and smells when it is hungry, a starter that has consumed its food source and is in need of feeding. It was alive!

WITH A LITTLE more research, I found that lactobacilli and wild yeasts both are hardwired to recognize when they are in mortal peril, and they release spores before their demise. These spores (kind of like eggs or seeds) can survive inhospitable environments, including harsh temperatures, until the coast is clear. At that point, they hatch and begin reproducing to create a brand new community.

YOUR BREAD ITSELF becomes an ecosystem of beneficial organisms—one that, unlike yogurt, is plant-based rather than animal based.

SO NEXT TIME you take your Franken-bread out of the oven, you can hold it in the air and cackle, "It's alive! It's alive!" Or you can just eat it, but where's the excitement in that?

14

2

GETTING "STARTED"

H·O·U·S·I·N·G, F·E·E·D·I·N·G, & USING N·A·T·U·R·A·L Y·E·A·S·T

Getting "Started"

"You're growing bacteria in our fridge. That's gross."

"Well, that bacteria is making our bread, so make friends."

"With your start?"

"His name is Peeta."

"You're crazy."

LUCKY FOR MY HUSBAND, "crazy" also feeds our family. Yes, I name my starts. When I was first teaching myself to bake with natural yeast, I had a knack for neglect. I tried giving my starts strong names to make up for that, but it didn't work. William (the Conqueror) I, II, and III all wasted away in the back of my fridge. Pepito and Phillip had promising beginnings but ended up in the drain as well.

THE STARTS I USE TODAY are named Peeta and Gale. The fact that those names are characters in the Hunger Games book series is mostly coincidence. Okay, so it's no coincidence, but highly appropriate, don't you think? They are well-fed and active, and make the most delicious loaves.

CALEB POINTED OUT to me that all my starts have been "male." Really, I don't know why. I guess that's because they provide for my family. Maybe because my starts are as hardworking as all the men in my life, so it fits. Who knows?

THE IMPORTANT THING is the mentality. My starts are more to me than just bacteria taking up space in my fridge. They're re-frigerated pets.

COWS MAKE MILK, chickens make eggs, and starts make bread. Simple as that.

CLUING IN TO THAT mentality is one of the things that helped me stop killing my starts.

A PET THAT ISN'T FED or cleaned up after doesn't last very long. They end up mean or dead. Starts are the same. Neglect your start for too long and it will go sour in a hurry and take its revenge on your loaves. The good news is that in this case, Old Yeller can be cured. With a few rare exceptions, most mean starts will sweeten up with a day or two of "powerfeeding."

SO WHAT EXACTLY DOES IT TAKE TO CARE FOR A START?

- **CONTAINER**
- **REFRIGERATOR**
- **REDUCE AND FEED EVERY THREE DAYS**

EASY, RIGHT? Let's break each step down into some-thing that can work for you.

17

How do I get my own starter?

A Greek woman once asked her mother where she got her starter, to which the mother replied, "From my mother." The woman then asked where her grandmother had gotten her starter. "From her mother," was the reply. The woman then asked, "Well, what do you do if you don't have a grandmother or mother to give you a starter?" The mother, appalled at the very idea, brusquely answered, "Then you don't bake bread!"

If we were living in a different time or place, this would be true for us too. But there are more than a few ways to get your hands on a starter. Caleb and I give starts away when we teach natural yeast baking classes. You can watch TheBreadGeek.blogspot.com or Caleb-Warnock.com for a schedule of our classes. You can also make your own, but it is not the option we suggest for beginners. Just as it is easier to find your destination in a familiar town, it is easier to create a new, healthy starter if you already have experience with one.

So here are a few options for getting your hands on a starter that will work for you.

Look Local

We guarantee you will be surprised by the number of people you know around you who currently have starters or know someone who does. Getting a start from someone local is the easiest way. One word of caution with this approach: If possible, sample some bread made with the starter you are considering "adopting." Ask yourself these questions:

1. Does it raise bread well?

2. Is the flavor to your liking? (Too sour, too mild?)

If the answer to both of those questions is yes, you're good to go. One tablespoon of a friend's starter (wet or dry) is all you need to grow your own pet. (If you can get more, ¼ cup of wet starter is ideal). Melissa once made the mistake of adopting a friend's starter and adding it to her own without sampling, and she paid the price. The starter was sick, or out of balance, and totally unable to raise bread. Once combined, the damage was irreversible, and she had to dump it out and start over with a new starter from a more reliable friend's pet. If a friend gives you dry starter flakes, follow the reconstitution instructions below.

What to do with your starter

For Dry Starter Flakes

If you have one tablespoon of starter:
Mix starter and ¼ cup water in small container until starter is dissolved.

Add ¼ cup (heaping) flour and mix until combined.

Cover and place in refrigerator, then read Basic Care and Feeding instructions on page 22.

For Wet "adopted" starter

If you have 1/4 cup of starter:
Mix starter and 1 cup water in a quart container until starter is dissolved.

Add 1 heaping cup flour and mix until combined.

Cover and place in refrigerator, then read Basic Care and Feeding instructions on page 22.

ORDER BY MAIL

The authors will mail free natural yeast starts to anyone who purchases this book.

To get your free natural yeast start, email your request to calebwarnock@yahoo.com. You will then receive an email from the authors with instructions for receiving your starter.

There are also a few reliable businesses that will send you starters at little or no cost to you. Mail-order starts from these sources usually contain a few tablespoons of dried starter flakes along with instructions for how to reconstitute them. Here are two sites we've used with great success:

FREE NATURAL YEAST OFFER

MILD STARTERS:

LDS HEALTH TODAY
www.ldshealth.ning.com

Or send a self-addressed, stamped envelope and a monetary contribution to

ORIGINAL FAST FOODS
1221 N 1270 E
American Fork, UT 84003

Melissa's mild starter originated with the LDS Health Today starter, which is said to be a documented 200-year-old family strain. We're not sure what constitutes a monetary contribution, but a small donation of a dollar or two would likely suffice.

SOUR STARTERS:

CARL GRIFFITH'S 1849 STARTER
www.carlsfriends.net

Send a self-addressed, stamped #10 (business size) envelope to:

OREGON TRAIL SOURDOUGH
P. O. Box 321
Jefferson, MD 21755

These starters will come with their own instructions for getting started, so follow those instructions before reading our Basic Care and Feeding instructions on page 22.

MAKE YOUR OWN

The reason we offer this option last is that it is the most time-consuming option and also has a variable success rate. Trying to begin a starter that is strong and has good flavor can be enough to make a person give up on natural yeast altogether. It is not impossible; people do it every day. But we do recommend familiarizing yourself with what a healthy starter looks and smells like before embarking on creating your own. Newborn starts can be a little finicky at first until their organisms reach a working balance.

Experimenting with starter creation is much less stressful when your ability to make bread doesn't depend on it in that very moment. You'll be more forgiving with yourself if you fail and much more willing to try again.

We recommend beginning with a starter that is strong and well-established. Learn what a healthy starter looks and smells like. Bake with it, become familiar with the science of starters. Then, armed with an arsenal of knowledge and experience, experiment to your heart's content!

Ready to attempt your own starter culture? I came across the following flowchart on a bread website called The Fresh Loaf (www.thefreshloaf.com) that is, in my opinion, the best and easiest guide to culturing a starter. It was created by forum contributor Arzajac to help people along their path to starter success. To view this file online, visit www.andrewzajac.ca/files/sd4.png, or search "starter flowchart" on The Fresh Loaf website.

Most important, the key to success in culturing a new starter is patience!

If multiple attempts have left you empty-handed, try adding crushed organic grapes or the peels of organic apples to the initial mixture, removing them once the bubbles start. Many people have had success with these methods.

New starters can often be delightfully sour. If you wish for a milder flavor, simply keep your starter in the refrigerator once it is established, and feed it regularly.

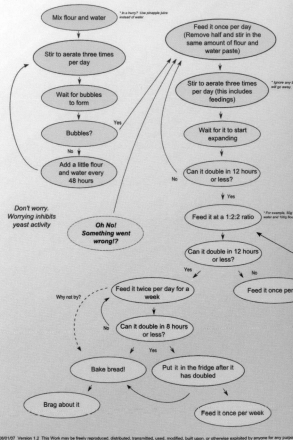

BASIC CARE AND FEEDING

HOUSING

FAQ: *What do I keep my starter in?*

ANSWER: Starts can be housed in just about anything designed to hold liquids. Tupperware, mixing bowls, small tubs, or canning jars are all great options. I use wide-mouthed canning jars. I like my containers to be see-through so I can get a good view of all the "activity" you can't see from the top, and with glass, I don't have to worry about any funky plastics or metals getting leached into my starter.

*IMPORTANT: Remember that feeding your starter will double its volume, then it will rise considerably while it "eats" in the fridge. Choose a container that will allow your start to grow without creating a "yeast bomb." Yes, I'm speaking from experience.

Active starts can survive on a countertop or in the fridge. Dormant starts are either frozen or dried into flakes. I keep Peeta and Gale in the fridge, with backup flakes in a resealable plastic bag tucked between the pages of my favorite bread book.

Caleb grew his yeast in a glass canning jar for several years before he was at an auction one day and found an authentic, historic pioneer yeast crock up for bid. He won the crock for 35 dollars at the auction, and his yeast loves it. It actually grows better in the crock than any other container he's tried. He thinks this might be because the crock insulates the temperature of the yeast, making it less vulnerable to the natural temperature fluctuations in a room that can affect Tupperware or glass jars.

FAQ: *Can I store my starter in metal containers?*

ANSWER: Not recommended.

Starters are acidic by nature, and prolonged contact with any container made of base metals (copper, brass, aluminum, or just about any metal other than stainless steel) can allow the starter to leach unpleasant deposits from the container. This is not a problem with stainless steel, but it is better to err on the side of caution and avoid storing your starter in metal altogether. Stirring your starter with a metal spoon (even if it's not stainless) or mixing your dough in a metal bowl (like the KitchenAid bowl) will not harm you, your starter, or the utensil.

FAQ: *Does my container need to "breathe"?*

ANSWER: Yes.

Starters require oxygen to survive. Most of that comes from what you mix into the starter when you feed it, but the container should never be airtight. Not only that, but as your starter grows, it releases CO_2, and an airtight container left too long unattended could become a "yeast bomb." For canning jar lids, simply flip the lid upside down before screwing on the ring to prevent a seal being made. Melissa has used a piece of plastic wrap or cheesecloth held down by a canning ring or rubber band as well.

FEEDING YOUR START

You will be feeding your starter twice a week, three to four days apart.

Pick two days out of your week to set in stone (more or less) as the days for feeding and using your starter. If Wednesday is the day you want to make bread, your next feeding day would be Sunday (or Tuesday and Saturday, Monday and Friday, and so on.) To feed your start, you will mix:

1 part starter with 1 part water and 1 part flour

Feeding your starter will double its volume. Feeding one cup of starter will give you two cups of starter to keep in the fridge. I have two cups of starter in my container at all times. One of those cups I keep to feed and grow, the other I use for baking.

Here is how you would feed one cup of starter:

MIX: 1 cup starter with 1 cup water

ADD: 1 heaping cup flour

Mix well, cover, and place in fridge.

The consistency we're aiming for is a lumpy pancake batter or runny oatmeal consistency. After a few feedings, you may get the "feel" of the consistency of your start and not need to measure so precisely.

NOTE: Underfeeding your start can give it an unpleasantly tangy flavor, so be sure to add enough flour.

Typically, you will feed your starter on the same day you use it in a recipe. A portion of your starter will go into your recipe, and you will simply feed what starter you have left. We'll go into more depth on this in the baking section coming up next.

Whether you have adopted a starter, reconstituted one from mail order, or started your own, this process begins after your starter has been growing in your fridge for three to four days.

When I pull my starts out of the fridge to use or feed them after a few days, I occasionally find a thin layer of liquid and darkened yeast on top. If you check out our "Anatomy of a Start," you'll see that the darkish, alcoholic-smelling liquid is, in fact, alcohol mixed

FAQ: *How do I know if my start is healthy and I'm feeding it enough?*

ANSWER: A healthy starter should double in volume between feedings. It should produce nice big, happy bubbles inside and minimal liquid on top. Put a rubber band around your starter container at the level of your recently fed start. In 24 hours, check it. Has it doubled in volume? If the answer is "almost," then you're in the clear. If not, and it continues to be lazy over the next few feedings, consult our troubleshooting section on page *** for ideas on rejuvenating your starter.

FAQ: *Can I freeze my start?*

ANSWER: Yes.

Starters can survive freezer temperatures for up to one month. At the end of the month, take your starter out, bring it to room temperature, feed it, and put it in the fridge or freezer.

with excess water from the last feeding. Don't ask us if you can drink it—we're not that brave. (We should give it a try one of these days though, since we can probably make more money off a Natural Yeast Ale Book than a bread book. Maybe we'll consider it for a companion series.)

Starts, like all other living things, create waste. As your start "eats" the food you provide, wheat "waste" will rise to the top. If you feed your start regularly, there may not be enough to notice, but the longer you go between feedings, the more noticeable it becomes.

The alcohol and darkened yeast are not harmful to you or your start, but it is a sign that your start is using up its food supply. Here's my system when I take Peeta and Gale out of the fridge to feed them:

1. Pour off any liquid.

2. Scrape off visible darkened yeast (it's okay if you don't get it all).

3. Measure out starter for recipe or dump in compost if you're not baking.

4. Pour remaining start into clean container (or reuse same).

5. Feed.

THE STARTER THAT
TOOK OVER THE HOUSE

Reducing your starter is very important. The best way to reduce your start is to bake with it, but that's not always possible. Every time you feed your start, you double its volume. If I started with one cup of start, feeding it would make two cups of starter. Feeding those two cups would make four cups of starter. Without frequently using or reducing your starters, you would very soon have enough starter to fill the fridge, the car, and the house.

I keep two cups of starter in my container all the time. One cup I keep to feed and grow, the other I use for baking. When it's time to reduce and feed, I use one cup for bread or crepes and then feed the other cup of starter and put it back in the fridge. If you don't have time to use it, then dump it in your compost or down the drain.

It is better to dump starter down the drain than postpone feeding until you have time to use it for cooking. I have soured many starts with that kind of thinking! Reducing and feeding together takes me ten minutes tops, every three days. I'd like to see you spend that little time taking care of any other pet (husbands included). As far as commitments go, it's really not asking much.

FAQ: *Do I have to use a clean, sterilized container every time?*

ANSWER: No.

The ecosystem of a starter is completely inhospitable to unfriendly or harmful bacteria. While your starter is alive and well, nothing harmful will grow inside your container. You may see chunks of dried starter on your container walls. These can be scraped off and stirred back in, or saved in a plastic baggie as "backup flakes." I use the same container for extended periods, and I appreciate the lack of extra dishes. If you ever see anything fuzzy or multi-colored (blue, green, black, and so forth) in your container, do not bother putting your starter in a new container. It is dead. Dump it out, wipe your tears, slap on a smile, and start over!

BAKING

Okay, so now you know how to feed and care for your refrigerated pet. Now let's get to the good stuff, where your start goes to work for you.

Of all the traditional methods I've used for baking bread, this is the least time-consuming. In a nutshell, we will be preparing dough, setting it to "soak" for at least six hours, shaping it for a final two-hour rise, and baking. The best part is, the six-hour soak happens while you are sleeping, working, or watching reruns on your sofa. All you have to do is mix it, shape it, and bake it.

After feeding, refrigerator starts need at least 24 hours to build up the right amount of yeast for raising bread. After that, the starter is good to use in bread for up to three days. Using a starter that hasn't been fed for four to five days can make bread that is very strong in flavor.

Make sure to stir down your start before measuring. You want to measure as few bubbles as possible, so really give it a good stir before pouring it into the measuring cup.

Here are two example schedules for how you will be using your starter:

TO BAKE
Thursday morning:

WEDNESDAY NIGHT
Mix up dough
Cover and set on counter
Go to bed

THURSDAY MORNING
Shape loaves and put into pans
Let rise two hours
Bake

TO BAKE
Wednesday evening:

WEDNESDAY MORNING
Mix up dough
Cover and set on counter
Go to work, play, school

WEDNESDAY NIGHT
Shape loaves and put into pans
Let rise two hours
Bake

Remember to feed your refrigerator start at least twenty-four hours before mixing up the dough in any schedule.

BUILDING & REDUCING YOUR STARTER

BUILDING YOUR START

If you're planning on working yourself up into a baking frenzy, you're going to need more than just one cup of starter. It is very easy to build starter volume.

Here's a suggestion for increasing your starter successfully.

Determine how much starter you have and how much starter you will need in the next few days. You will increase your starter simply by increasing the amount of water and flour you feed it,.

THE NO-RUSH, REFRIGERATOR METHOD

At each normal feeding day, double the amount you would normally feed your starter until you have as much starter as you need (don't forget to use a bigger container!).

EXAMPLE:

1 cup starter

2 cups water

2 heaping cups flour

This would give you 3 cups of starter: one to keep and feed and two to bake with, which is enough to bake 8 loaves of bread. If you need more than 3 cups, do the same at the next feeding:

3 cups starter

6 cups water

6 heaping cups flour

Your starter may need an extra day or two to process all this new "food" and get nice and strong. You will now have 9 cups of starter, and a lot of baking to do!

THE HURRY-UP COUNTERTOP METHOD

Take one cup of your starter and transfer it to a larger container (Feed the other cup and return it to the fridge.) Feed the transferred starter four times the normal "food" amount.

EXAMPLE:

1 cup starter

4 cups water

4 heaping cups flour

Cover the container and leave it on the countertop for 6–12 hours. When it has stopped bubbling and rising, it is ready to use.

NOTE: It can be helpful to put a rubber band around the container to mark the level of your starter right after it has been fed. Once it has doubled in size, it is ready to use.

FAQ: *Can't I just build it up all at once? Why do I have to go slowly?*

ANSWER: You could try . . . but I couldn't guarantee the results. I have tried to build my own starter too fast, and sometimes it works, but other times it throws off the balance of the whole start. It can take some time for the starter to work its way through all the new "food." Not only that, but every time you add new flour and water to the starter, you also add new bacteria to the mix. Your starter needs time to compensate for the new additions and stay strong. If you use your starter before it is evenly distributed and strong, you may end up with bread that doesn't rise and a weakened starter.

REDUCING YOUR START

There are times when I know I will not be using my starter for a few weeks and don't want to waste flour by feeding a starter. In this case, I will simply measure out ¼ cup, dump out the rest, feed it (¼ cup water, heaping ¼ cup flour) and maintain it at that size. Do not take your starter down below one tablespoon. Less than one tablespoon is not enough to sustain life for your starter for very long.

CONSISTENCY & TEMPERATURE

CONSISTENCY

Those of you who have baked with starts before will wonder why we recommend a thick pancake batter consistency in this cookbook. Starts are adaptable things. I have used starts ranging in consistency from fairly liquid to clay-like. The thicker a start, the stronger the flavor it tends to have. In our recipes, we are going for a rather mild flavor. As a result, our recipes are measured to fit a liquid start. If you would like to increase the flavor of your bread, and you have some experience in baking, thicken your start over a few feedings. When you bake with it, don't forget to reserve some of the flour to compensate for the extra in your start. Check our blogs for additional information sources if you would like to experiment further with your start.

TEMPERATURE

I highly recommend keeping your start as an exclusively refrigerated start. Refrigerated starts are easier to care for and more versatile in baking than countertop starts. Countertop starts tend to have a stronger sour flavor and require two or more feedings a day. I love a good sourdough, so for me this is no problem when it comes to artisan breads and rolls. Sweet doughs, however, are less compatible with sour starts.

VACATION

One of the main concerns I hear from people is what they are supposed to do with their starters when they go on vacation. The first question I ask them is, "How long will you be gone?" One week of vacation will not do irreparable damage to your refrigerated start. Just make sure to feed it right before you leave. Friends with starters will often "starter sit" for you while you're gone, or they can give you some of theirs when you get back if your starter dies while you're away. But let's say you'll be gone for a month (or more) with no sitters or replacements nearby. Your options are to freeze your start (up to one month, then simply defrost and feed) or make dried starter flakes to reconstitute later.

MAKING STARTER FLAKES

So how exactly do you make dried starter flakes, you ask? Not hard at all.

1. Start with a drying surface—a cookie sheet, parchment paper, or silicon mat—that can be kept out of the way during the drying process.

2. Feed your start and leave it on the counter for a few hours (no more than four).

3. Pour as much of the starter as you would like to dry onto your surface.

4. Use a spatula or rubber spreader to create a thin, even coat of starter across your surface.

5. Allow your starter to dry for 12 to 24 hours. When it is completely dry, it will crackle and flake at the slightest touch.

6. Put your flakes into a resealable bag and crunch them up until you have small flakes in your baggie. This will make measuring your dried starter easier when you need to use it.

7. Label your bag with name and date ("Gale, 2/17/2012") and store in a dark cupboard or refrigerator

Some people make flakes by collecting the dried dough or starter clinging to the sides of starter containers or mixing bowls. Both ways are effective; one simply provides more flakes than the other.

Please make sure that your start is absolutely dry, or you may end up with inedible "blue cheese" flakes.

RECONSTITUTING STARTER FLAKES

To reconstitute your starter the process is equally simple.

1. Measure out some flakes. You can use as little as a "pinch" or as much as a tablespoon, depending on how much you have on hand.

2. Dissolve the flakes in ¼ cup water.

3. Add ¼ cup flour, stirring vigorously to incorporate plenty of air into the mixture.

4. Let sit undisturbed on the counter for two to four days. By the fourth day, your mixture should be beginning to "bubble" and grow.

5. Transfer your start to a larger container (if necessary) and feed it ½ cup water and ½ cup flour. Put it in the fridge and continue feeding as normal. (See page 22 for Basic Care and Feeding instructions)

6. **NOTE:** If your starter has NOT bubbled up by the fourth day, try this: Stir your starter well, then measure out ¼ cup. Dump out whatever is left in your container, then return the ¼ cup of starter to the container and feed it ¼ cup water and ¼ cup flour. Let it sit on the counter for another few days. Once it's bubbling, feed it ½ cup water and ½ cup flour and stick it in the fridge!

HELPFUL HINT: *If you are going away for a few days and want to bring your starter with you, here is a recommendation. Take a portion of your starter and transfer it to a new container, creating a "clone" of your current starter. Feed both your current starter and the new clone, then leave your current starter at home. Keep your travel starter in a refrigerated lunch box or something similar until you get to a refrigerator. This minimizes the chance that you will permanently damage your only starter while traveling. I have had so many instances of this happening since I started teaching classes and taking Peeta with me everywhere I go. I just can't care for his "needs" the way I should when out and about. Now I just leave him at home and clone him when I need a big batch of starter for a class. That way if something goes wrong, I don't have to worry!*

TROUBLESHOOTING

POWER-FEEDING

Sometimes our starts get a little under the weather. They stop bubbling up nicely when fed, and loaves don't rise quite as high. In most cases this happens when a start has been neglected too long or the yeast population of the starter has gotten out of balance. In either case, the key is power-feeding. The idea is to flush out any irregularities in the start's makeup over the course of a few days. Here's the steps for power-feeding an ailing start:

1. Pour off any liquid and spoon off any darkened yeast.

2. Transfer ¼ cup of your start into a clean container.

3. Add ¼ cup water to your clean container. Stir to dissolve starter.

4. Add ¼ cup flour.

5. Place start in fridge for 24–48 hours.

Watch your starter until it has stopped bubbling and growing or has started to form a layer of dark liquid at the top. Depending on how "sick" your starter is, this could be a matter of days or hours. Now you will feed the start again, without reducing or using what you already have.

1. Pour off any liquid and spoon off any darkened yeast

2. Measure how much starter you have, then return it to the container.

3. Add an equal amount of water (example: ½ cup starter=½ cup water). Stir to dissolve starter.

4. Add an equal amount of flour.

5. Cover and place starter in fridge for 24–48 hours.

Repeat this process until you have 2 cups of starter. You should see a significant improvement in your starter by now. If your starter is still floundering at this point, reduce it to ½ cup and start the process again.

Remember! Once you get the hang of caring for your start, you will rarely need to use this process. Whatever happens, remember to be patient with yourself and your starter.

BOOSTING YOUR START: WARM-UPS

Fridge temperatures are not always as stable as a person might think. Temps can rise and fall depending on whether tomorrow is grocery day (the fridge is empty), yesterday was grocery day (the fridge is full), or how many times the kids open the doors to tell you there's nothing to eat.

My starters tend to gravitate toward the back of the fridge between uses and feedings, and that is prime real estate for occasional frostbite. A deep chill or light freeze won't hurt your start, but it can bring activity to a screeching halt. A starter with minimal activity can still be used for making non-rising breads like crepes, pancakes, waffles, cake, or any other recipe that calls for baking soda or powder. The yeasts are still at work breaking down wheat, they just can't move fast enough to raise bread.

If your starter has gotten very slow and lazy about raising bread, feeding-time warm-ups are a good option. Around the time you will be feeding your start, or when you are baking with it, allow it to sit out on the counter for an hour or two (no more than two). In that short time span alone, you should start to see a distinct rise in activity. Little bubbles should form within an hour.

These short warm-ups once or twice a week will allow your starter to get warm enough to increase activity without getting so warm that it will start to produce the bacteria that will give your starter a more sour flavor. Of course, if you want a more sour flavor, extended warm-ups will do the trick.

PROBIOTIC BOOST
(FOR MILD STARTS)

My friend Nancy has a long history of healthy, happy starts. Her secret? Once a week she adds the contents of a probiotic pill to her start. While probiotics can be pricey, they last a long time when used for start-boosting, and they don't add much to the overall cost of your bread. Nancy believes that the lactobacilli in the probiotic help keep the good bacteria in your start healthy. This method also helps maintain a mild flavor in your start. I have had more success with warm-ups and power-feeding than with probiotics, but I have seen probiotics work in the starters of friends.

THE PINEAPPLE BOOST
(FOR SOUR STARTS)

I consider the pineapple boost a last-ditch effort only because it requires a trip to the grocery store. I have used this method with tremendous success to rejuvenate starts that responded to nothing else. This method is successful because it alters the pH, or acidity, of your start, making it an environment unfriendly to any strains of bacteria that aren't good for bread-making.

NOTE: Changing the acidity of your start can also affect the flavor. I do not recommend this method for those who do not enjoy a more sour flavor in their start.

For this method, all you need to do is use pineapple juice instead of water when feeding your start. Whenever I boost my starts, I leave them on the counter rather than in the fridge so I can watch their progress, and cut down the size of my start so I'm not using up too much flour with the increased number of feedings. Here is an example of my schedule for a typical boost:

DAY 1:
Mix ¼ cup start with 2 tablespoons pineapple juice. Add a scant ¼ cup flour, cover, and leave on counter.

Before bed—if start has doubled and started to recede, repeat the process.

DAY 2:
Same as day 1

DAY 3:
If your start is happy and bubbling, return to normal flour/water feedings and then, before bed, put your start back in the fridge. If your start is still struggling, try pineapple for one more day. If your start is not back on its feet by day 4, and you've tried both power-feeding and the boost, I'm afraid you're out of luck.

I discovered this method on my favorite bread website, The Fresh Loaf, when my start suddenly refused to raise my bread anymore. After a week of experimentation, followed by sweet success, a forum contributor asked me, "Why don't you just start over? You do have backup flakes, don't you?" That's when I did the face-palm. How could I have forgotten my flakes? All this time I'd been laboring to avoid sending Gale down the drain when I had backup flakes the whole time. Just a reminder that the best time to make flakes is when your start is performing its best. You never know when you'll need them!

Avoiding the
Super-Massive Failure

ONCE UPON A TIME, there was a woman who loved her family. She was so passionate about keeping them healthy that she decided to do everything in her power to feed them right. She took up baking, got a starter, studied food, cooked food and baked bread. Then one day she stopped what she was doing and looked around her. The starter was dead. The bread was flat. The food was burned. Her children (when she finally found them) were next door eating Twinkies. She brought them home and threw out the starter, the bread, and the food. She opened a chocolate bar, snuggled her kids, told herself she just wasn't cut out to be one of those women, and vowed never to do anything healthy ever again. The End.

Or it almost was, except I had really come to believe in the health benefits of this bread. So why, if I had been trying so hard to do everything right, had everything gone so terribly wrong? My husband's answer to this question was infuriatingly accurate:

"Multitasking isn't the key to everything in life, Melissa. Keep it simple."

At first my pride was hurt. As a wife and mother, how on earth could I accomplish anything without multitasking? Was I doomed to failure? He, of course, had a much more rational explanation.

"Take your bread, for example. It seems to me that the most important thing is keeping your starter healthy. Start there. When you figure that part out, move on."

This from the man who almost had me committed the day I named my starts. But he was right. The effort I had been making previously was valiant, to be sure, but lacking one very important thing. Sustainability. I had taken on so much, so quickly that I had set myself up for inevitable, super-massive failure. I would have given up that day in the kitchen if I did not have such a strong commitment to what I believed naturally yeasted bread could do for the health of my family. So I got my priorities back in order and decided to learn to bake this bread one success at a time.

And guess what, it worked.

Baking with a starter is not the easiest thing you could do with your time. If it were, there would be no market for rapid-rise yeast and store-bought bread. But if you believe in this bread the way I do and have any kind of life responsibilities at all (job, kids, husband, exceptionally needy cat . . .) then this schedule just might help you avoid the super-massive failure in your life.

NOTE: If you are a natural master of adaptability (unlike me), this schedule may not be necessary for you. For you talented, daring souls, feeding your starter once or twice before jumping into baking

32

may be all you need. This schedule is merely a contingency plan for those of us who require a little more "settling in."

MONTH ONE

(Yes, I said month.) Practice feeding your start. No baking. Simply find your starter rhythm and make it harmonize with the music of your life. Using the feeding instructions on page 22, pick two days a week to be your feeding days and *stick to it* for the entire month. Don't be discouraged by the amount of unused starter going down the drain. If you keep one cup of starter, you will have used eight cups of flour during this feeding month. You can "waste" that same amount in one failed two-loaf batch of bread. Perspective is key.

You can also use this "practice" time to fill your intellectual arsenal. Learn what you can about your new pet. Attend classes, read blogs, and talk to other bakers. Stay motivated by surrounding yourself with people and information that will excite you about your developing skill.

MONTH TWO

On one or both of your feeding days, use the leftover starter that would normally go down the drain to make crepes, pancakes, or waffles. These recipes are important to master early on, because they are the recipes you will find most useful during this

learning curve. If and when your starter hits a lull and struggles to raise bread, these recipes will allow you to continue to use your starter while you get it healthy again.

MONTH THREE

Now you're ready for the big time. Pick one of your feeding days that will now become a dough day. You will use your starter to set up dough so it will be ready to bake in the morning or evening. On your nonbaking feeding day, use your excess starter to make pancakes, crepes, or waffles as usual.

At the end of month three, you should be prepared to bake for your family without putting life on hold and with little or no waste. The best part is, this schedule is customizable to your needs and can be used at any time during your baking years. Sometimes life gets out of hand and there is no way to make bread a priority. During those times, go back to month one. Just feed your start and wait for life to slow down. When you're ready, move on to month two, or skip right to month three. You are in control.

There may be bumps along the way and times when, for what seems like no reason at all, things don't work out. That's not called failure—it's life as we know it. So don't give up. Take a step back, take a few breaths, and give it another try. With small, determined steps, your destination will always be success!

KNOW THE DOUGH

A QUICK GUIDE FOR KNEADING BY HAND AND WORKING WITH WHOLE WHEAT DOUGH

WHEN I WAS LEARNING to bake, no one was around to teach me. I relied on the Internet and books, but before YouTube and other video-sharing sites, it was difficult to learn from written instructions alone. By happy mistake, I stumbled upon *The Laurel's Kitchen Bread Book* at the library. The opening chapters detailed the process of baking in word and picture more clearly than I had ever seen it before. Laurel taught me to bake. While only three or so of her recipes use natural yeast, her book stands as the leading official on how to bake whole wheat bread in the bread world. (The fact that I know this, and that I just used the phrase "bread world" is proof of what a bread geek I really am.)

In this section, I will pass on what I have learned from her and other bakers, as well as some discoveries of my own for all you brute-strength hand-kneaders out there and all those who just want to learn a little more about baking whole wheat bread.

GLUTEN

Baking with whole wheat flour can be a challenge. Perfect whole wheat loaves will take some practice, but understanding the mechanics of the substance you're working with will make things easier.

First off, let's talk gluten. Gluten is a protein found in wheat. It is the binding force that allows wheat flour to be made into an elastic dough. Without gluten, bread dough would look like cornmeal. When wheat flour is mixed with wet ingredients, the gluten binds together in a tangled, unorganized mass. Kneading untangles the gluten strands, strengthens them, and weaves them into a "parachute" that will lift and raise your bread.

With whole wheat dough, the fibrous roughage that is beneficial to our digestive tract can also pose challenges to baking. The bran and endosperm (which are removed from white flour) take longer to absorb moisture and can work against the gluten in binding. Here are some tips that will help you work with your dough.

MIXING

Mix dry ingredients together in a large bowl. Use your spoon to create a "well" in the center of the flour.

In a separate bowl, mix starter, water, and any other wet ingredients the recipe calls for. Pour wet ingredients into the center of your dry ingredients "well."

Stir liquids with a spoon or dough whisk (see page 158), slowly incorporating dry ingredients as you stir, until all the flour is mixed in and you have a shaggy mass of dough.

DID I ADD ENOUGH FLOUR?

Now it's time to get your hands dirty.

For hand mixing, the best time to predict a good outcome for your kneaded dough is just after you've mixed all the ingredients together into a shaggy mass of rough dough. Grab a handful of the stuff and squish it between your fingers. Does it resist your pressure? Do you have to strain at all to get it to squeeze through? If so, your dough is too dry.

On the other hand, if the dough is running down your arm or liquid squeezes out between your fingers, your dough is too wet. The happy medium is to have dough with enough flour to give cohesion without stiffness.

Many people mistakenly think that firmer dough makes well-formed loaves. In fact, the moisture in the bread contributes as much to the cooking process itself

With whole wheat flour, floured surfaces for kneading or shaping bread can be problematic. As I said earlier, whole wheat flour takes longer to absorb moisture than white flour. It is very easy to add too much flour to whole wheat bread without realizing it. Working whole wheat dough on a floured surface can quickly reduce moisture levels in your bread, making it difficult for the bread to rise properly in the oven.

The solution to this problem is moisture. When it comes to bread in general, "wetter is better," and the same applies to the bread in this cookbook.

Now you don't want your bread dough running off the edge of your table, but *slightly* wet is easier to bake than *slightly* dry.

I use water when working with my dough exactly like I would use flour. I put a little bowl off to one side, wet my hands, and lightly spread water across the surface I will be working on. The basic idea is to create just enough of a water "barrier" to keep your dough from sticking to the work surface. As with flour, I sometimes need to add more water here and there across my surface or to my tools when the dough starts to stick. Again, you want a barrier, not a bath.

For white dough, flour works as a great barrier, although the finest French chefs consider the use of flour "cheating."

TECHNIQUE

There are almost as many varieties of kneading techniques as there are bakers in the world. Some are more efficient than others. All kneading techniques will require two things some people are not willing or able to give: time and energy. At this stage in my life, I save those priceless commodities for my small children, so I use a mixer. When I do feel like getting my hands dirty, or my daughter begs to be my "baker" (meaning my baking-helper), I choose one of two kneading techniques to get the job done .

as the external heat does. As the temperature of the oven rises, moisture in the bread will heat and steam, giving the inside of the bread its fluff and sponginess. It is for this reason that you should not slice into a hot loaf of bread. The internal steam is still cooking. Cut it open and you lose the "finishing" stage of bread baking. This is one of the reasons that dry dough turns out flatter, denser loaves.

KNEADING

We're almost ready to knead, but before you start, here's some important information. If you have worked with white bread dough before, you are familiar with the phrase "on a lightly floured surface," right?

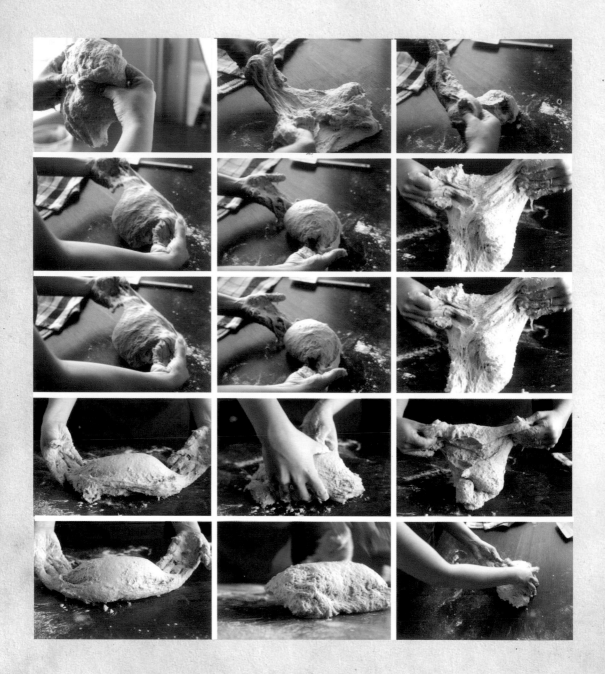

TECHNIQUE #1
FRENCH SLAP AND FOLD
(and Melissa's current favorite)

This method is delightfully aggressive and a great method for working tension out of yourself and your dough. The next time you're in a spat, whip up a loaf using this method. It could save your relationship. And what better way to make up than over a slice of hot bread? Fighting has never been so delicious.

STEP 1
With dough in the "shaggy mass" stage, place it on your work surface with no water or flour. That's right, none. Be brave! This method starts out a little messy, but the dough cleans itself up as it develops.

STEP 2
With both hands palms-up, slide your fingers under your dough from the right and left sides, leaving thumbs on top.

Lift the dough off the table so your thumbnails are facing you. Swing the bottom of the dough up and away from you, then slap it down hard on the work surface. When I say hard, I mean *hard*! Let it really smack the table. It should be so loud, pets and small children will run for cover. *That* loud.

STEP 3
Your hands should now be thumbnails-down on the table. With the bottom half of the dough stuck to the table, stretch the dough up and over itself, basically folding it in half away from you.

Pull your fingers out from between the folded dough.

STEP 4
Repeat the first three steps until the dough has smoothed itself out and can pass the windowpane test (see windowpane test section on page ***).

TECHNIQUE #2
STRETCH AND FOLD
(least abrasive)

This process will put absolutely no pressure on sensitive wrists and is a great option for someone with the time but not the strength for kneading. Using this method with whole wheat dough will not achieve maximum fluffiness but will still produce nice loaves. One of the purposes of kneading is to introduce air into the structure of the dough. While this method will develop the dough nicely, you will not get as much air into your dough as with the French Slap and Fold or a mixer.

STEP 1

Follow the recipe you are using to the point where you have created a rough, shaggy mass of dough. Place the dough in a bowl and then cover it with a damp towel, plastic wrap, or plate.

Allow the dough to rest for 45 minutes.

STEP 2

Using your hand or a soft dough scraper, pull the dough out of the bowl and onto your work surface. Water on the work surface isn't necessary but can help keep dough from dirtying your countertop too much.

Gently stretch and pat the dough out until it is about ⅓ the original height. As you stretch out your dough, gently rub out any flour pockets that didn't get mixed in with your dough. This process can be damaging to the dough later on, so get it all done now!

STEP 3

Fold your dough as you would a letter, the top third down, and the bottom third up. Then fold the right third in, followed by the left. You should now have a tight "packet" of dough. Place the dough in a bowl, cover, and let rest for 45 minutes.

STEP 4

Repeat steps 2 and 3, skipping the italicized portion.

STEP 5

Repeat steps 2 and 3, skipping the italicized portion.

STEP 6

You have now had four 45-minute rests, and three stretch-and-folds. At this point your dough should look smooth and elastic. Follow the remainder of the recipe for shaping and baking.

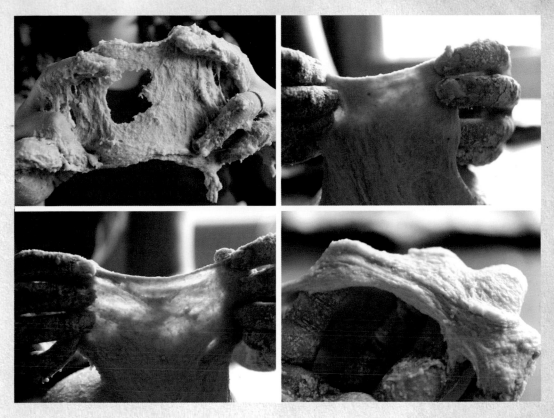

THE WINDOWPANE TEST

When hand-mixing dough, it can be difficult to tell when you're "done," especially if you're out of shape and your arms feel like jumping off your body for a break after ten minutes. The easiest method I've found of deciphering dough doneness is the Windowpane Test.

Take a small section of your dough, about the size of a quarter in diameter. Gently stretch the dough between the thumb and forefinger of both hands, creating a small square "pane" of dough. Finished dough will create a smooth pane that can be stretched thin enough

to be translucent when held up to a light. There should be no tears, and the dough should look uniform. I kind of like to think of it as what you see when you look at a pane of stained glass.

If your dough tears before it can be stretched thin enough to be translucent, more kneading is needed. Be patient with yourself. Efficient and effective kneading is a skill developed with practice and patience. The more you bake, the quicker your dough will develop as your kneading improves. Plus, just think of the amazing upper-body workout you're getting for free. Go you!

RESTING

Most people don't have time in their busy schedules to allow their dough the luxury of a rest (especially if the baker isn't getting any), and since you can turn out perfectly good loaves without long rests, I omitted that part of the professional process. If, however, you do have an extra 20 to 30 minutes available to you, resting your dough can make hand-kneading easier.

There are two stages at which resting can benefit your dough.

STAGE 1:
THE SHAGGY MASS STAGE

Once you have mixed all the dry and wet ingredients into a shaggy mass of rough dough, cover the bowl and allow it to rest for 20–30 minutes.

Here's why resting at this stage can be helpful:

When wheat berries pass through a grinder, they explode under the pressure of the grinding wheels. Flour then is basically a powdery collection of wheat shrapnel. Kneading wet flour that has not been given the chance to soften can take more work. It takes longer for the dough to strengthen enough for the gluten to withstand its own abrasiveness. The tiny bits of "shrapnel" in your dough can tear at the gluten strands your hands are working so hard to develop. Giving your dough a rest gives the flour a chance to fully absorb the

moisture and soften, speeding up the kneading process. So mix up your dough, grab a snack, and hit the couch for a quick read, chat, or television show. Your wrists will thank you!

STAGE 2: SHAPING

The second rest is right before final shaping. After the long rise, gently remove your dough from the bowl onto a damp surface. Use a dough scraper or serrated knife to separate the dough into as many loaves as you are planning to bake. Cover your dough on the counter and allow it to rest for ten minutes while you grease your pans or baking sheet.

After the long rise finishes the development of your dough, its gluten strands are aligned in the dough much like a muscle. Similarly, the more the dough is handled, the more tense it becomes. Picture yourself sitting relaxed and warm in a comfortable place. Now imagine someone throwing open the door and yanking you to your feet, determined to teach you the polka. Feeling a little tense? Maybe confused by my analogy *and* tense. In either case, your dough empathizes completely.

Cutting and separating is stressful for your dough. Tense, stressed-out dough resists rolling and shaping. Give your dough a little "alone time" to recoup from the shock of being chopped in half, and your job will be much easier.

PROOFING

Proofing, in bread terms, is the process of allowing your dough to rise for a period of time. Our dough proofs only twice. One 6 to 24 hour proof, and another final proof in the pan (or on a baking sheet).

The first proof is completed when the dough has doubled in size and when it has been proofing at least six hours. This is not the case with all bread doughs, and not even with all sourdoughs. The difference with our dough is that we are using the first proof as an autolyze. An autolyse is also known as a predigestion, but that sounds less appetizing, so we'll stick with the first.

An autolyse is the oh-so-critical process of bread-making that neutralizes harmful enzymes, breaks down the negative aspects of gluten, and frees up vitamins and minerals for human digestion. Animals that naturally thrive off grains have multiple stomachs to accomplish this. Seeing as we have only one wimpy gut to accomplish two to three times the work, it's no wonder digestive illnesses and grain-based intolerances are so common. On the other hand, I can barely manage the one gut I've got, so I'll stick to the autolyse and let the cows have all the triple stomach fun.

Since the final proof comes right before the bread is baked, it is important not to let your dough over- or under-proof. This proof is complete when the dough has doubled in size. Most dough will proof in 1½–2 hours in a warm (75 degrees) place. Controlling your bread's environment as much as possible during the final proof is helpful to turning out beautiful loaves. A simple solution for this controlled environment is proofing your dough inside your oven with only the oven light on. I live in a cold winter climate, so sometimes I will turn my oven on to "warm" for a minute or two, then turn it off, leaving the light on and placing my pans inside to let the dough rise.

CAUTION: Placing your dough in an oven or other space that is too warm (85+ degrees) can cause the dough to rise quickly and over-proof.

Over-proofing happens when your dough has risen too long, creating air pockets under the top "skin" of your dough and weakening the texture. The dough loses some of its elasticity and, when baked, yields loaves that are uneven and sometimes crumbly.

Under-proofing is what you get when (for whatever reason) your dough never doubles before baking. Sometimes I get impatient, sometimes it's too cold, sometimes my start is lazy; there are many reasons for under-proofed dough. More often than not, my dough under-proofs because of temperature or lack of patience.

BAKING

I have read any number of techniques for deciphering the "doneness" of a baked loaf of bread. I have yet to find a technique more precise than a good old food thermometer. Simply pull your loaves out of the pan when your timer goes off and insert the thermometer into the bottom of the bread. When your thermometer reads 190 degrees, the bread is done. Easy, right? Since I was never a very proficient bread "thumper," this technique works best for me.

Before you even get out the thermometer, here are a few other easy signs that your bread is not quite finished. Bread loaves pull away from the pan as they near completion. If your loaf still clings tightly to the pan on all sides, it's probably not done (assuming you remembered to pre-grease your pans). The same process that tightens up your loaves also firms up the crust. If you attempt to turn a loaf out of the pan and the crust is indenting at your touch, it is not finished baking yet. In either case, just put the loaves back in for another five to ten minutes or until the thermometer reads 190 degrees.

DOUGH ENHANCERS

LET'S TALK GLUTEN. When you get into the world of whole wheat baking, gluten is something you hear quite a lot about: how to strengthen it for bread making purposes, how to neutralize it for digestive purposes, and on and on. Natural yeast baking with its long fermentation process is a great answer to many of those questions.

When we bake with a starter, we are providing a moist, acidic environment that will tame the gluten over the course of six to twelve hours. At the same time, we are also giving the dough a chance to rise and organize its gluten strands into webbing that will make excellent bread.

I have had people ask me why, if starters can do all this for gluten, I am not a fan of adding Vital Wheat Gluten (a dough enhancer) to my whole wheat bread. Almost all whole wheat recipes nowadays call for vital wheat gluten to improve fluffiness and texture of whole wheat loaves.

Well, I don't add dough enhancers to my bread because I don't have to. The bread I make with these recipes is light, fluffy, and delicious without special (and expensive) additives.

Second, I'm not completely sold on the health aspect of many of these products. In the news we are constantly hearing arguments for and against certain grains, legumes, and other natural products. Take for example the great soy debate. Some people say soy is a vicious, evil substance very possibly imported from Lucifer himself. Others tout it as a wonder-food and miraculous cure-all (halo sold separately). What I have learned in my research regarding this topic and many others is that the food or substance in its raw form is rarely the problem.

Increasing amounts of research are finding that grains and legumes are not constructed like multivitamin tablets. You cannot simply add this vitamin, remove this mineral, or isolate this protein, package it, and sell it all on its own. Why?

Let's try this analogy: think of a grain like your local gym. You have weights for strength building, cardio for heart health and weight loss, yoga for focus, and Zumba just for fun. What if you isolated only the weights area and ignored the rest of the gym? What if you went a step further and got rid of everything except upper-body weights? In a month or two you would look like a breed of hairless gorilla. Not so pretty. Many athletes have suffered serious injury from focusing too heavily on one muscle group without strengthening the muscle groups that support it. Grains function in much the same way.

The design of a grain is such that each component is vital to the function of the others. There are enzymes within grains that benefit from the strength of the proteins, while simultaneously compensating for the protein's weaknesses. By isolating gluten, you are also separating it from the components designed to help it do its work most effectively with the fewest negative side effects.

The same argument goes for commercial dough enhancers. I'm all for adding additional whole food products to your bread to enhance texture and flavor. Flax seed, coconut oil, buttermilk, eggs, and malt are all great examples of this. I am not such a huge fan of chemically engineered or extracted products that are largely unknown in their makeup or health implications.

Really, I could go on forever about this topic. It applies to so many aspects of food science and is a problem that stems from food science getting a little too big on itself. I have found that in almost all cases, nature knows its business better than we do.

I want to bake bread in a way that allows nature to do her job without interference from me. So no gluten, no commercial dough enhancers. Just whole food goodness and a little faith in Mother Nature.

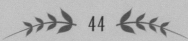

Between a Rock and a Hard Place
The Nitty-Gritty on Grinding

GRINDING IS PROBABLY the least time-consuming part of making my bread. With an electric grinder, I can fill the hopper, start the grinder, and work on something else until the machine is finished. No special trips to the store for flour, no bags of pre-ground flour waiting to go rancid. I simply grind as much flour as I want, when I want it. When you bake as much as I do, that's a beautiful thing.

If you are going to be grinding your own flour, here are a few things you need to remember:

THE NOSE KNOWS

The shelf life of your flour will depend greatly on the climate where you live. If you have an inkling your flour may be too old, just put your nose to it. One whiff should let you know if the oils in the flour have gone bad. If you're not sure, best to throw it out. Baking with rancid wheat is a waste of time and money.

Whole wheat flour will not store for years in your pantry like white flour. Store-bought whole wheat flour will go rancid within three months. Freshly ground flour will expire even sooner.

Wheat berries contain small amounts of oil, mostly housed in the germ of the wheat. The oil is what goes rancid over time and spoils the flour. White flour doesn't have the germ in it, so it stays fresh for centuries. Like Twinkies. This is why labeling for whole wheat bakers is such an important part of your process (see following section). You may be grinding flour from a grain you seldom bake with. Or you might grind enough flour to last for a

few weeks, then take a spur-of-the-moment trip to Cancun instead. It could happen. So don't forget to label your flour.

IT'S ALL IN THE LABEL

When it comes to grinding flours from more than one kind of grain, the key is to label, label, label! Color coding is not enough. I have often found myself standing over two grain buckets thinking "Was the orange lid for wheat or spelt? Well, spelt has darker color, so it must be in the orange bucket. No, wait . . ."

I love using painter's tape (available at hardware stores) to mark my buckets and bins, because it comes off easily if you need to empty a bucket and use it for something else. Labels should look something like this:

FOR GRAINS:
Hard Red Wheat

Purchased 4/23/2011, Macey's
(purchase location*)

FOR FLOUR:
Soft White Wheat

Ground 4/23/2011

Including the purchase location is not critical but can be useful in the event you have a question or complaint about the flour you are using.

TRIPLE CLEAN

When it comes to wheat (or any grain, for that matter), three is the magic number. If possible, buy wheat that has been "triple cleaned" from a reputable production company. Grinding stray

45

rocks that make their way into your grains will ruin your machine, and most grain mill companies will not honor warranties of machines that have ground rocks.

Wheat is not a very expensive grain to purchase, so I buy mine directly from the Bosch store near my home as a precaution. The wheat is not any better in quality, but I know that the manager is vigilant about the cleanliness of the wheat that comes into his store.

OXIDATION

Within twenty-four hours of being milled, whole wheat flour loses as much as 45 percent of its nutrients to oxidation. And in only three days, up to 90 percent of the nutrients are lost. If you must grind ahead, store your flour in the freezer when possible. This will at least slow down the oxidation process and, in some studies, has been found to improve baking quality.

For myself, I grind flour that is stored for feeding my starts and then grind fresh flour for baking.

GRAIN TO FLOUR RATIO

When grinding your own wheat, it can be helpful to know how much grain you will need to grind the flour needed for the recipe. Quantity can vary slightly with different grains, but as a general rule

1 cup grain yields 1½ cups flour

MIX IT UP: MULTIGRAIN FLOUR

Did you know you can grind more than one kind of grain at a time? For some reason, I had never considered creating multigrain flours until it was suggested to me. Create your own custom blends to expand the nutritional buffet your bread offers to nibblers.

CAUTION: keep gluten-free grains (such as amaranth and quinoa) to a maximum of 25 percent of your flour content to preserve your bread's ability to bind and rise.

HAND GRINDERS

I'm not gonna lie. I do not have the patience or the time for hand grinders. I have known people who use them exclusively and love the workout, but they're just not for me. I've considered buying one for emergency situations, but I'm banking on the fact that I have a genius husband who I will force to construct a bike-powered generator on such an occasion. That's how badly I don't want to hand-grind my own flour. You may feel differently, and if you do, go you! (I have to say that because you could probably beat me up with those hand-grinding biceps of yours.)

3

GETTING YOUR
BREAD GEEK ON

· T · I · M · E · TO · B · A · K · E ·

ADAPTING
NON-STARTER RECIPES

ONE OF THE VERY FIRST questions asked in my very first natural yeast class was this: "I have a bread recipe—an old family favorite. Will my starter work with that?" Since that first class, I have rarely taught about natural yeast without that same question coming up at some point. In most cases, I've tried to take the time to look over the recipe myself, note any adjustments, and see if it is starter-friendly.

Not all recipes will work with a starter if they were created during the commercial-yeast era and tailored in taste and time restraint to that type of baking. Some recipes simply cannot be adjusted, but the vast majority can.

This small section is an invitation to explore the jungles of the wild yeasts (another geeky name for natural yeast). This is not a quest for immediate and effortless perfection but an opportunity for the bold and daring to see how far they can go in the adventure of baking with natural yeast. Not all recipes will be successful, but you will find that the more open you are to experimentation, the more easily you will be able to predict the recipes that will succeed, and the more often your results will render a tasty reward.

RATES OF EXCHANGE

When working with other bread recipes, you may have noticed that one teaspoon (or packet) of commercial yeast is usually the prescribed amount for raising one loaf of bread. In some cases (usually quick-rise breads) that amount will be higher, but the general consensus is one teaspoon per loaf. Because of the variety of commercial yeasts available, some with different rising

capabilities, we base our starter adaptations on the number of loaves being prepared, not the quantity of commercial yeast used.

For naturally yeasted breads, we bake with ¼ cup of starter per loaf of bread. Some naturally yeasted recipes are designed to use more or less starter, but ¼ cup per loaf is the standard.

A NOTE ABOUT
HYDRATION

The starter we instruct you to keep in *The Art of Baking* is called a 100-percent hydration starter. This means that our starter is equal parts flour and water (by weight, not volume). A starter with lower hydration (like 50 percent) would resemble more of a dough, while a starter of higher hydration (like 150 percent) would resemble cake batter. Our starter goes right down the middle, with a runny oatmeal consistency.

This information is important to know for two reasons. The first is that in most cases, adding a 100-percent hydration starter to a recipe will not affect the texture, because you are adding an equal amount of flour and water to the recipe. Unless you are working with a very stiff dough, the starter is neutral to changing the wetness or dryness of a dough.

The second reason to know our starter's hydration is in the event that you wish to use it in a sourdough recipe from another cookbook. The sourdough recipe you wish to use will tell you what hydration of starter the ingredients are measured for. If our starter is too wet for the recipe you want to use, don't worry. There are plenty of instructions on the Internet for adjusting the hydration of your starter to fit what you need.

BASIC GUIDELINES: SPOTTING THE RIGHT RECIPE

You already know that the starter works in the recipes included in this cookbook. Spotting an easily adaptable recipe can be as simple as identifying whether or not the recipe you want to use has a similar dry/wet ratio as those that already use natural yeast.

Here's an example:

EVE'S BREAD
(from *The Art of Baking*)

INGREDIENTS

½ cup starter

2½ cups water

2 tsp. salt

5–6 cups flour

YOGURT BREAD
(made up in my head just this second)

INGREDIENTS

2 tsp. active dry yeast

½ cup warm water

1 cup plain yogurt,

1 cup water

4 cups whole wheat flour

1½ cups oatmeal flour

2 tsp. salt

Do you see the wet/dry similarities? Eve's bread has a flour content of 5–6 cups, the yogurt bread has 5½ . Eve's bread has 2½ cups of water, the yogurt bread has 2½ cups of total wet ingredients.

This recipe is perfect for starter adaptation. In most cases, recipes that are similar to thse in our cookbook within a cup or so of wet/dry ingredients will work. Keep in mind that our recipes are all formulated for a two-loaf yield. You may want to adjust a recipe for only one loaf. In that case you would simply look to see if the recipe you are looking at is approximately half the wet/dry measurement of one of our recipes.

Here are some additional tips when adapting new recipes.

1. Make sure to add all the flour to the dough before the long rise. This is the only way to make sure that your bread will be 100 percent nutritionally available to you when you eat it.

2. Try to stick with cultured dairy. Buttermilk, yogurt, and kefir are great options for cultured dairy in recipes. If you are baking something with a sweeter or subtle flavor, use a vanilla- or maple-flavored yogurt. I've never had dairy spoil in a recipe, but better to be safe than sorry.

3. Eggs are okay. Baking kills salmonella (as does hand soap), so bread doughs with eggs in them are the salmonella equivalent of cookie dough. I have had lengthy forum discussions with bakers all over the world about the possibility of eggs spoiling in a dough left out to rise overnight, and the consensus was that no one had ever seen that happen. The one thing they did agree on was that if it ever did spoil, you would smell it before the dough made it near the oven. Rotten eggs are not timid.

4. Start with the familiar. I recommend that your first attempts at adaptation be with recipes you are already familiar with. The reason for this is that you already know the consistency and texture of the dough you will be working with, and you will know if you are off the mark.

5. Use the baking powder or soda the recipe calls for. If you are adjusting a muffin, pancake, or cake recipe, simply sprinkle it over the dough in the morning and mix it in. I recommend this only because the texture of what you are baking will change notably by leaving them out, and you may not be as pleased with the result.

Above all, remember to be forgiving with yourself, and don't be surprised if it takes two or more attempts to get the mixture just right (especially for more complicated recipes). Remember, you are working with a living, breathing group of organisms, and the fact that you are able to put them to work in your own recipes is just plain awesome!

4

THE BASIC SIX

RECIPES FOR EVERYDAY BAKING

EVE'S BREAD

Basic Whole Wheat Sandwich Bread

When Eve whipped up the first post-Eden loaf, her recipe probably looked a lot like this. The ingredient list is short, using only basic items that could be stored long-term for food storage or hauled across the country in a wagon. I like to think of this as Crisis Bread: the nutrient rich, complex carb food source I could make for my family in a state of emergency. This delicious and mild bread has a wheaty sour flavor, and it is a good base for any herbed or savory bread.

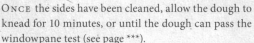

INGREDIENTS

½ cup start (stir before measuring)

2½ cups lukewarm water

2 tsp. salt

5–6 cups whole wheat bread flour

SETTING UP THE DOUGH
(At least 10 hours before baking)

COMBINE start, water, and salt in mixer.

ADD 5 cups of flour, then continue adding flour until dough "cleans" the sides of your mixer bowl. (There may be residual bits near the top, and here and there along the sides, but the lower half of the bowl should be clean.)

ONCE the sides have been cleaned, allow the dough to knead for 10 minutes, or until the dough can pass the windowpane test (see page ***).

DAMPEN a large work surface with water and pull the dough out of the mixer bowl onto your work surface. (You want just enough water to keep the dough from sticking, but not enough to waterlog your dough. See page *** for more instructions on kneading with water.)

WET your hands with water, and knead the dough a few times, until the texture is uniform.

PLACE dough smooth-side up into a pregreased bowl or container. Remember to choose a container that allows your dough room to double in size. You can also split your dough and use two smaller bowls.

COVER your bowl with greased plastic wrap or with a thick, damp kitchen towel (thin towels dry out too quickly and stick to the dough).

PLACE bowl on countertop to rise overnight (or all day) for 6–12 hours.

FEED your start, and place in refrigerator.

SHAPING AND FINAL RISE

AFTER a minimum of 6 hours, turn dough out of bowl onto wet work surface.

WET hands and use dough scraper or sharp serrated bread knife to cut the dough into 2 equal pieces.

SET pieces aside on a damp surface and grease your pans. (This gives your dough time to "relax" before shaping.)

TAKE one dough section and pat it out on your damp work surface.

SHAPE each piece individually into sandwich loaves, artisan boules, or rolls (shaping tutorials on page ***).

ALLOW the loaves to rise in a warm place for 2–2½ hours, or until the dough slowly returns a gentle fingerprint.

PREHEAT the oven to 375 degrees.

BAKE for 25 minutes, or until a thermometer inserted into the bottom of the loaf reads at least 180 degrees.

REMOVE from pans and allow to cool completely before cutting.

53

ADAM'S BREAD

Caleb calls this "Adam's Bread" because it's faster to make than Melissa's "Eve's Bread" and that's why Caleb likes this recipe. He uses whole wheat flour ground fresh at home, but white flour or half-white, half-whole wheat will also work. Using bread flour will result in the lightest loaf. (During the rest and rising periods in this recipe, Caleb found the best success by turning the oven on to preheat at 350 degrees for 20 seconds, turning off the oven, and placing the dough inside. During the long rising period, repeat this 20-second warming at the halfway point).

INGREDIENTS

3 cups natural yeast starter

4 cups flour

2 tsp. salt

2 cups room temperature water

STEP ONE

WITH a wooden paddle or spoon (or KitchenAid or Bosch mixer), combine ingredients until the resulting wet dough is thick and elastic, about five minutes. Let dough rest in a warm spot for five minutes.

ADD ½ cup flour at a time (kneading until dough is no longer sticky). This step is likely to require quite a bit of flour, perhaps three cups or more. Knead for a total of 8–10 minutes, until the dough becomes a smooth ball.

STEP TWO

ALLOW dough to rise 3–4 hours, until doubled in size, occasionally sprinkling a few drops of water over the top of the dough to keep the surface moist, if necessary.

STEP THREE

DIVIDE the dough in half, shape into loaves, and place in buttered, floured loaf pans. Allow dough to rise until doubled, about 90 minutes. Bake for 30–40 minutes at 350 degrees. For a crunchier crust, bake at 450 degrees for 10 minutes, then reduce temperature to 350 for 20–30 minutes. Serve hot with butter and preserves.

54

HONEY MOLASSES SANDWICH BREAD

This recipe is a step up from Eve's bread. I've added some sweeteners that neutralize any sour from the yeast. The sweeteners we use are high in nutrients and easily stored. Why honey and molasses? Mostly, because they taste really, really good. Plus I've got an overactive sweet tooth. Should you need more convincing, there's health benefits too (see our blog for more info). This bread can woo even the most adamant whole wheat snubber, like my friend Loraine, who "does not like wheat bread" and yet is disappointed when I show up to her house without a loaf of this particular bread.

INGREDIENTS

½ cup start (stir before measuring)

2½ cups lukewarm water

2 tsp. salt

¼ cup honey*

¼ cup molasses

7–8 cups whole wheat bread flour

*The quantity and type of sweetener can be adjusted as needed. If you are increasing the honey or molasses, be sure to increase your flour by about double the measured amount of the sweetener.

SETTING UP THE DOUGH
(At least 10 hours before baking)

COMBINE start, water, salt honey, and molasses in mixer.

ADD 7 cups of flour, then continue adding flour until dough "cleans" the sides of your mixer bowl. (There may be residual bits near the top, and here and there along the sides, but the lower half of the bowl should be clean.)

ONCE the sides have been cleaned, allow the dough to knead for 10 minutes, or until the dough can pass the windowpane test (see page 41 for more information).

DAMPEN a large work surface with water and pull the dough out of the mixer bowl onto your work surface. (You want just enough water to keep the dough from sticking, but not enough to waterlog your dough. See page 37 for more instructions on kneading with water.)

WET your hands with water, and knead the dough a few times, until the texture is uniform.

PLACE dough smooth-side up into a pregreased bowl or container. Remember to choose a container that allows your dough room to double in size. You can also split your dough and use two smaller bowls.

COVER your bowl with greased plastic wrap or with a thick, damp kitchen towel (thin towels dry out too quickly and stick to the dough).

PLACE on countertop to rise overnight (or all day) for 6–12 hours.

FEED your start, and place in refrigerator

SHAPING AND FINAL RISE

AFTER a minimum of 6 hours, turn dough out of bowl onto wet work surface.

WET hands and use dough scraper or sharp serrated bread knife to cut the dough into 2 equal pieces.

SET pieces aside on a damp surface and grease your pans. (This gives your dough time to "relax" before shaping)

TAKE one dough section and pat it out on your damp work surface.

SHAPE each piece individually into sandwich loaves, artisan boules, or rolls (shaping tutorials on page 123).

ALLOW the loaves to rise in a warm place for 2–2½ hours, or until the dough slowly returns a gentle fingerprint.

PREHEAT the oven to 375 degrees.

BAKE for 25 minutes, or until a thermometer inserted into the bottom of the loaf reads at least 180 degrees.

REMOVE from pans and allow to cool completely before cutting.

GRAMMY'S BREAD

My Grammy suffers from a condition that prohibits her from eating anything that metabolizes into sugar. Anything. Fruit, carbohydrates, and standard sweeteners are all on the list. But guess what? She can eat this bread. The lactobacilli and wild yeasts in the starter feed on simple sugars, breaking them down into a form her digestive system can handle without freaking out. It is very nearly identical to Eve's bread, but with one significant addition: coconut oil.

Coconut oil is good for us in about ten million ways (if you don't believe me, Google it). It is a good source of healthy fats, provides beneficial vitamins and nutrients, and also aids the body in the digestion of sugar. Coconut oil has a natural sweetness to it and can imperceptibly lighten the flavor of a loaf.

INGREDIENTS

½ cup start (stir before measuring)

2½ cups lukewarm water

2 tsp. salt

1 Tbsp. coconut oil

5–6 cups whole wheat bread flour

SETTING UP THE DOUGH:
(At least 10 hours before baking)

COMBINE start, water, salt, and coconut oil in mixer.

ADD 5 cups of flour, then continue adding flour until dough "cleans" the sides of your mixer bowl. (There may be residual bits near the top, and here and there along the sides, but the lower half of the bowl should be clean.)

ONCE the sides have been cleaned, allow the dough to knead for 10 minutes, or until the dough can pass the windowpane test (see page 41 for more information).

DAMPEN a large work surface with water and pull the dough out of the mixer bowl onto your work surface. (You want just enough water to keep the dough from sticking, but not enough to waterlog your dough. See page 37 for more instructions on kneading with water.)

WET your hands with water, and knead the dough a few times, until the texture is uniform.

PLACE dough smooth-side up into a begin bowl or container. Remember to choose a container that allows your dough room to double in size. You can also split your dough and use two smaller bowls.

COVER your bowl with greased plastic wrap or with a thick, damp kitchen towel (thin towels dry out too quickly and stick to the dough).

PLACE on countertop to rise overnight, (or all day) for 6–12 hours.

FEED your start, and place in refrigerator

SHAPING AND FINAL RISE

AFTER a minimum of 6 hours, turn dough out of bowl onto wet work surface.

WET hands and use dough scraper or sharp serrated bread knife to cut the dough into 2 equal pieces.

SET pieces aside on a damp surface and grease your pans. (This gives your dough time to "relax" before shaping)

TAKE one dough section and pat it out on your damp work surface.

SHAPE each piece individually into sandwich loaves, artisan boules, or rolls (shaping tutorials on page 123).

ALLOW the loaves to rise in a warm place for 2–2½ hours, or until the dough slowly returns a gentle fingerprint.

PREHEAT the oven to 375 degrees.

BAKE for 25 minutes, or until a thermometer inserted into the bottom of the loaf reads at least 180 degrees.

REMOVE from pans and allow to cool completely before cutting.

We already know that coconut oil is good for us in lots of ways, but did you know that it also works as a dough enhancer? The first time I used coconut oil in a loaf, it was because I had run out of olive oil. You'd be surprised how many of my greatest discoveries have been the result of a poorly stocked pantry and a little culinary creativity.

I expected that the bread would taste coconut-ty but decided to go ahead anyway. When the bread came out of the oven and I served up the first slice, there was no hint of coconut, and the bread was softer than any I had ever baked before. Some breads are soft in a fall-apart kind of way, but this bread was soft and strong, the best kind.

Coconut oil can be used in any of our basic bread recipes, but I do not recommend it for breads that you want to have a more savory flavor.

Since my family does not have any sugar-related conditions, I make Grammy's Bread with ¼ cup honey per two-loaf batch. It is by far my favorite sandwich bread.

59

BREAD MACHINE RECIPE

This recipe is roughly half starter to begin with, and with the two rises typical to the bread machine process, it will have four hours of rises in which the fresh flour can be worked upon by the natural yeast. Notice that this recipe calls for a one cup of white flour. You can make this bread using only whole wheat flour, but the loaf will be much fluffier if you add just one cup of white flour.

INGREDIENTS

1½ cups starter

1¾ cups lukewarm water

2 Tbsp. butter

1 Tbsp. raw honey, or 2 Tbsp. grocery store honey

2½ cups whole wheat flour

1 cup white flour

1¼ tsp. salt

MIX all ingredients into a bowl roughly together with a spoon until just incorporated.

PUT the lump of dough into your bread machine and use as directed per your model.

60

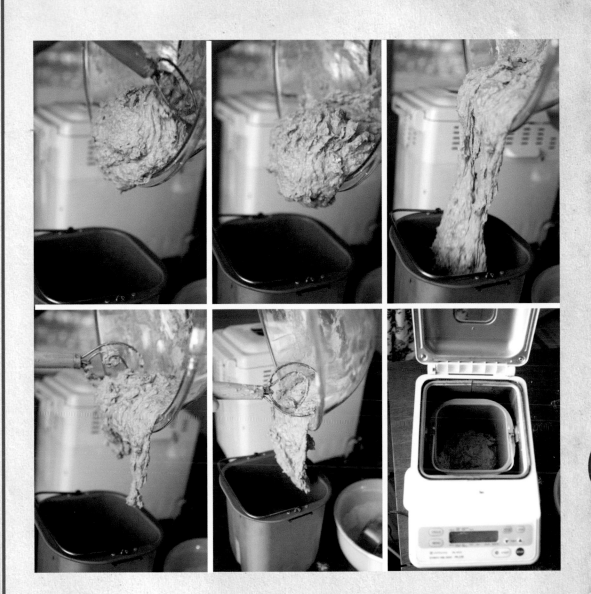

61

NO-KNEAD BREAD

When I first started baking, I mixed all my dough by hand. Considering how much I bake, it's no wonder my wrists rebelled. No-knead recipes can rescue the wrists of non-mixer bakers, no special talents required. I do prefer to knead my bread (now that I have a mixer) because I feel it makes stronger, prettier bread, but such things can seem like vain details when your time or wrists can't take the pressure of kneading.

INGREDIENTS

6 cups flour

2 tsp. salt

½ cup starter

3 cups water

¼ cup honey

MIX flour and salt together in a bowl. In separate bowl, combine starter, water, and honey. Create a "well" in the center of your dry ingredients like you would for potatoes about to be smothered in gravy.

POUR wet ingredients into your flour "well" and begin to stir slowly, letting the liquids pull flour from the sides and incorporate it slowly into the middle. Once all the flour has been mixed in, you will have a "shaggy mass" of dough.

DON'T be tempted to add more flour—this dough should be very sticky. The sticky wetness of this dough is what makes it work. Place dough into a pregreased bowl, cover, and set on counter overnight (or all day).

IN 6–12 hours, use a rubber scraper or other dough scraper to gently pull dough from bowl onto a lightly floured surface. Separate into 2 equal pieces of dough.

WITH floured hands, pat the dough out into a rectangle and shape into a sandwich loaf. Place loaf into pregreased bread pans. If the top of your bread looks a little mangled from the stickiness, lightly wet your hands and gently smooth out the top of your loaf until it looks prettier. Repeat with second loaf. Cover, and let rise 2 hours.

BAKE loaves at 350 degrees for 30–35 minutes, or until thermometer inserted into bottom of bread reaches 180 degrees.

IMPORTANT: If at all possible, do not open the oven for the first 25 minutes of baking. Wet doughs rely on consistent heat to cook out excess moisture in the dough. Opening the oven too many times can throw off the temperature and your dough's ability to rise well.

62

5

DRESSING UP
YOUR LOAVES

F·R·U·I·T·S, N·U·T·S, S·E·E·D·S, & S·P·R·O·U·T·S

DRESSING UP YOUR LOAVES

FRUITS, NUTS, SEEDS, AND SPROUTS are easy additions to any tasty loaf. Some-thing inside me inexplicably sighs when I sink my teeth into a buttered slice of walnut-date or apricot-pecan bread. Does that happen to you too? Assuming you said yes (if not, this moment of silence is for you . . .) you will be happy to know that making these beautiful breads is as easy as a scoop and a pour.

The following recipes will give you exact measurements and suggestions, but hopefully, you will find yourself wanting to experiment with your own flavors and additions. Here are some basic guidelines for embellishing your standard loaf.

As all of the recipes in this cookbook are for a two-loaf yield, I will assume you are mixing dough batches of that quantity. Double or half quantities as needed.

MIX IT UP

The best time to add fruit, nut, and seed embellishments to a loaf is during the initial mixing and kneading. This is the easiest way to incorporate them if you are using a mixer, and the healthiest. Nuts and seeds are similar to grains in their makeup. All require a lengthy soak to make them optimally nutritious. Adding them to the dough that will be soaked overnight kills two birds with one stone. If you are mixing by hand, it can be easier to soak the nuts and seeds separately overnight, then add them to the loaf during shaping, as in the cinnamon raisin loaf.

HOW MUCH?

My play-it-safe rule of thumb is this: Add no more than ½ cup TOTAL of fruits, nuts, or seeds to any one loaf. Too many additives can weigh down your bread, making it difficult to rise. Better to have a bread whose flavor leaves you wanting a little more than a fruity paperweight.

CHOP, CHOP

I don't recommend using whole nuts or large dried fruits in your loaves. These obstacles can make your bread difficult to cut or even eat at times. I prefer to coarsely chop all nuts and larger fruits (like apricots or dried apple slices). This will give your bread pockets of pure pecan in every slice, or bursts of whatever flavor you're attempting.

Grinding your nuts or seeds into powder will flavor your loaf in a different way. This will add a consistent, nutty flavor to the entire loaf. CAUTION: Do not add more than ¼ cup of any nut or seed powder (or flour) per loaf. Doing so will compromise the dough's ability to hold together and maintain elasticity.

Remember, these guidelines are meant to be a jumping off point for your own creativity. Be bold, try new things, and when you do, send us your pictures!

WHOLE WHEAT CINNAMON RAISIN BREAD

This bread is very versatile. My husband has a genetically inherited sweet tooth and loves starting the day with a little something sweet. I started making this bread especially for him, but let's just say it benefits the whole family. It makes delicious toast and wonderful French toast. We figured that out by happy accident when we ran out of bread one Sunday morning. It's almost a disappointment to make French toast any other way around our house, and it will be at yours too once you give it a try.

INGREDIENTS

whole wheat honey molasses dough (page 56), proofed overnight (or all day) and ready for shaping.

1 Tbsp. butter (softened)

raisins ½ cup, or to taste

cinnamon (to taste)

REMOVE dough gently from bowl and divide it in half.

ROLL or pat the dough out into a rectangle. It should be no wider than your bread pan, and the dough should be no thinner than ¼ inch after rolling.

SPREAD the softened butter evenly across the rectangle. More butter can be added, but remember that too much butter can turn your bread into a giant cinnamon roll, which while tasty, can come apart when sliced.

SPRINKLE cinnamon and raisins across your rectangle. Pat them lightly into the dough so they don't move around too much when you roll the dough up.

WORKING from one short end to the other, begin rolling up the dough so that the finished roll will fit easily in your pan. Once rolled, pinch the dough along the seam to seal it, tuck the ends under, place it in the pan, then cover and set it on the counter for the final rise (2 hours or until doubled in size).

PREHEAT the oven to 350 degrees, and bake 25–30 minutes, or until a thermometer inserted into the bottom of the loaf reads 180 degrees.

HELPFUL HINT: *Leave a one-inch margin unbuttered around your rectangle. This will help keep butter and cinnamon from leaking out of your bread and burning on your pan.*

68

WALNUT DATE BREAD

This bread is delicious when used as a compliment to dinner, as a stand-alone dessert, or as French toast. The walnut and date portions here are merely a suggestion—feel free to experiment with them as you please. I am simply putting down here what is most likely to work in the structure of a loaf and for general taste. Some people like a lot of fruits and nuts into their bread, not minding that it does not rise quite as high or that the bread might break apart a little easier. Others might choose to finely dice their dates and crush their walnuts to powder so that the bread bears the taste without the chunks. In most cases, the dates will caramelize into the dough a bit (unlike raisins) so you will not find yourself chewing through chunks of dates.

INGREDIENTS

½ cup starter (stir before measuring)

2½ cups lukewarm water

2 tsp. salt

¼ cup honey

¼ cup molasses

1 Tbsp. olive or coconut oil (optional)

7–8 cups whole wheat bread flour

½ cup chopped walnuts

½ cup chopped dates

SETTING UP THE DOUGH
(At least 10 hours before baking)

COMBINE start, water, salt, honey, molasses, and oil in mixer.

ADD 7 cups of flour, then continue adding flour until dough "cleans" the sides of your mixer bowl. (There may be residual bits near the top, and here and there along the sides, but the lower half of the bowl should be clean.)

ONCE the sides have been cleaned, allow the dough to knead for 10 minutes.

WHILE the bread is kneading, prepare your dates and nuts. A few minutes before the end of kneading, dump your chopped dates and nuts into the mixing bowl.

WHEN the dough has been kneaded long enough to pass the "windowpane test" (see page 41), remove the dough and any loose fruit and nuts onto a slightly damp work surface. (You want just enough water to keep the dough from sticking, but not enough to waterlog your dough. See page 37 for more instructions on kneading with water.)

WET your hands with water, and knead the dough a few times, until the texture is uniform and the remainder of the fruit and nuts has been incorporated into the dough evenly. This can take a minute or two, so be patient.

PLACE dough smooth-side up into a pregreased bowl or container. Remember to choose a container that allows room for your dough to double in size. You can also split your dough and use two smaller bowls.

COVER your bowl with greased plastic wrap or with a thick, damp kitchen towel (thin towels dry out too quickly and stick to the dough).

PLACE on countertop to rise overnight (or all day) for 6–12 hours. Feed your start, and place in refrigerator.

If kneading the fruit and nuts into your loaves is too much work, simply add them to the loaf during shaping, much as described in the recipe for cinnamon raisin bread (page 68).

70

SHAPING AND FINAL RISE

AFTER a minimum of 6 hours, turn dough out of bowl onto wet work surface.

WET hands and use dough scraper or sharp serrated bread knife to cut the dough into 2 equal pieces.

SET pieces aside on a damp surface and grease your pans. (This gives your dough time to "relax" before shaping.)

TAKE one dough section and pat it out on your damp work surface.

SHAPE each piece individually into sandwich loaves, artisan boules, or rolls (shaping tutorials on page 123).

ALLOW the loaves to rise in a warm place for 2–2½ hours, or until the dough slowly returns a gentle fingerprint.

PREHEAT the oven to 375 degrees.

BAKE for 25 minutes, or until a thermometer inserted into the bottom of the loaf reads at least 180 degrees.

REMOVE from pans and allow to cool completely before cutting.

71

APRICOT NUT BREAD

This recipe stems from a breakfast porridge I fell in love with a few years ago and had to try in a bread. I love the strong sweetness of the apricots mixed with the creaminess of yogurt and a hint of coconut. Yum!

INGREDIENTS

½ cup starter (stir before measuring)

2 cups lukewarm water

½ cup plain yogurt or kefir

2 tsp. salt

½ cup real maple syrup

1 Tbsp. coconut oil

7–8 cups whole wheat bread flour

½ cup diced apricots

½ cup chopped nuts (walnuts, pecans, almonds, or a mixture!)

¼ cup shredded coconut

SETTING UP THE DOUGH:

(At least 10 hours before baking)

COMBINE starter, water, yogurt, salt, maple syrup, and oil in mixer.

ADD 7 cups of flour, then continue adding flour until dough "cleans" the sides of your mixer bowl. (There may be residual bits near the top, and here and there along the sides, but the lower half of the bowl should be clean.)

ONCE the sides have been cleaned, allow the dough to knead for 10 minutes

WHILE the bread is kneading, prepare your apricots, nuts, and coconut. I like to take my ¼ cup of coconut and pulse it once or twice in a food processor or blender to make it extra small. Some people love the flavor but not the texture of shredded coconut. A few minutes before the end of kneading, dump your chopped apricots, nuts, and coconut into the mixing bowl.

WHEN the dough has been kneaded long enough to pass the "windowpane test" (see page 41), remove the dough and any loose fruit and nuts onto a slightly damp work surface. (You want just enough water to keep the dough from sticking, but not enough to waterlog your dough. See page 37 for more instructions on kneading with water.)

WET your hands with water, and knead the dough a few times, until the texture is uniform, and the remainder of the fruit and nuts has been incorporated into the dough evenly. This can take a minute or two, so be patient.

PLACE dough smooth-side up into a pregreased bowl or container. Remember to choose a container that allows room for your dough to double in size. You can also split your dough and use two smaller bowls.

COVER your bowl with greased plastic wrap or with a thick, damp kitchen towel (thin towels dry out too quickly and stick to the dough).

PLACE on countertop to rise overnight, (or all day) for 6–12 hours.

FEED your starter, and place in refrigerator.

SHAPING AND FINAL RISE

AFTER a minimum of 6 hours, turn dough out of bowl onto wet work surface.

WET hands and use dough scraper or sharp serrated bread knife to cut the dough into 2 equal pieces.

SET pieces aside on a damp surface and grease your pans. (This gives your dough time to "relax" before shaping.) Take one dough section and pat it out on your damp work surface.

SHAPE each piece individually into sandwich loaves, artisan boules, or rolls (shaping tutorials on page***).

ALLOW the loaves to rise in a warm place for 2–2½ hours, or until the dough slowly returns a gentle fingerprint.

PREHEAT the oven to 375 degrees. Bake for 25 minutes, or until a thermometer inserted into the bottom of the loaf reads at least 180 degrees.

REMOVE from pans and allow to cool completely before cutting.

*If kneading the fruit and nuts into your loaves is too much work, simply add them to the loaf during shaping, much as described in the recipe for cinnamon raisin bread (page ***).*

For a little extra pizzazz, toss a small handful of chopped nuts and coconut in a little maple syrup and sprinkle on top of your loaves just before placing them in the oven. These will brown and crisp, creating a pretty topping for your bread.

73

SPROUTED WHEAT BREAD

This bread could easily be included in our artisan bread section, because it takes a little extra attention and skill than most of our other breads. This recipe is not an intensive tutorial on sprouting. Should you wish to sprout different grains for use in your baking, I recommend looking up sprouting instructions for that grain specifically. Soaking times vary depending on the size and density of a grain. Wheat takes a few days, and quinoa will sprout in one third the time.

This bread tastes wonderful, looks beautiful, and will have the neighbors "oohing" and "aaahing" at your incredible baking skills. Plus, it could not be more nutritious! It's bread and a salad all in one!

SPROUTING INSTRUCTIONS

Begin this 3 days before baking.

INGREDIENTS

½ cup wheat berries*

Quart canning jar (or something similar)

Nylon net or cheesecloth

Rubber band (to keep the cover in place).**

*If you don't grind your own wheat, wheat berries (grains) can be bought at most health food stores in the bulk section. Many groceries stores that have a bulk section usually carry wheat berries as well.

**Most health food stores carry "sprouting lids" for sprouting in jars. They are not expensive, come in small and wide-mouthed varieties, and are a good investment if you sprout frequently, because they are easy to clean.

RINSE the wheat berries and put them in a quart jar. Don't overload the jar— more than ½ cup gets crowded.

FILL jar with water and stir gently with a long utensil to release large air bubbles hiding in the berries.

PLACE nylon net or cheesecloth over the jar opening.

74

> *Sprouts are living things and need oxygen to survive. Never cover your sprouting container with a solid lid, or your sprouts will die. If you feel that the texture of your sprouts is too chewy for your taste, try steaming them lightly, then cooling them before adding them to your dough.*

USE a rubber band or the metal jar ring to hold the nylon or cheesecloth in place (or just put on your sprouting lid).

SET the jar aside to soak for 12 hours.

DRAIN the water thoroughly after 12 hours—shake a bit to remove most of the water. Rinse and drain the berries 2 or 3 times, draining well on the final rinse.

PLACE the bottle in a dark place where you will not forget about it.

RINSE the wheat berries with room temperature water every morning and night, then drain and put back in a dark place.

AFTER 36–48 hours, you should start to see little sprouts growing, like tiny tadpole tails.

ONCE the sprouts are visible, the sprouted berries can be used in baking. The longer the sprouts grow, the more bitter the sprout becomes (think wheat grass), so using your sprouts earlier as opposed to later is usually better.

BAKING THE BREAD

INGREDIENTS

½ cup starter (stir before measuring)

2½ cups lukewarm water

2 tsp. salt

1 Tbsp. olive oil

⅓ cup honey

6–7 cups whole wheat bread flour

½ cup sprouted wheat

SETTING UP THE DOUGH
(At least 10 hours before baking)

COMBINE starter, water, salt, oil, and honey in mixer.

ADD 6 cups of flour, then continue adding flour until dough "cleans" the sides of your mixer bowl. (There may be residual bits near the top, and here and there along the sides, but the lower half of the bowl should be clean.)

ONCE the sides have been cleaned, allow the dough to knead for 10 minutes. A few minutes before the end of kneading, add your sprouts to the mixing bowl and allow them to incorporate while the dough finishes kneading.

WHEN the dough has been kneaded long enough to pass the "windowpane test" (see page 41), remove the dough and any loose sprouts onto a slightly damp work surface. (You want just enough water to keep the dough from sticking, but not enough to waterlog your dough. See page 37 for more instructions on kneading with water.)

WET your hands with water, and knead the dough a few times, until the texture is uniform, and the remainder of the sprouts have been incorporated into the dough evenly. This can take a minute or two, so be patient.

75

PLACE dough smooth-side up into a pregreased bowl or container. Remember to choose a container that allows room for your dough to double in size. You can also split your dough and use two smaller bowls.

COVER your bowl with greased plastic wrap or with a thick, damp kitchen towel (thin towels dry out too quickly and stick to the dough).

PLACE on countertop to rise overnight (or all day) for 6–12 hours.

FEED your starter, and place in refrigerator

SHAPING AND FINAL RISE

TURN dough out of bowl onto wet work surface after a minimum of 6 hours,

WET hands and use dough scraper or sharp serrated bread knife to cut the dough into 2 equal pieces.

SET pieces aside on a damp surface and grease your pans. (This gives your dough time to "relax" before shaping.)

TAKE one dough section and pat it out on your damp work surface.

SHAPE each piece individually into sandwich loaves, artisan boules, or rolls (shaping tutorials on page 123).

ALLOW the loaves to rise in a warm place for 2–2½ hours, or until the dough slowly returns a gentle fingerprint.

PREHEAT the oven to 350 degrees

BAKE for 25 minutes, or until a thermometer inserted into the bottom of the loaf reads at least 180 degrees.

REMOVE from pans and allow to cool completely before cutting.

NANCY'S FLATBREAD

This bread was inspired by my friend Nancy Brook, who was one of the "gurus" on my path to natural yeast enlightenment. We could really have almost an entire section just on the varieties of flatbreads. My challenge to you with this bread is to be creative! Since this is a flatbread and does not have to rise, you don't have to worry so much about weighing down the bread. Add your favorite sprouts, seeds, nuts, and ground legumes. As a reference, I recommend a half cup of any embellishments per one loaf of dough. So for a two-loaf batch, one cup is a good guideline but could be increased for this flatbread.

INGREDIENTS

Any one of the Basic Six recipes plus . . .

1 cup (or more) of any combination of nuts, seeds, sprouts, or fruit.

Suggested Embellishments:

Sesame seeds	Pumpkin seeds
Poppy seed	Sunflower seeds
Kamut sprouts	Chia seeds
Rye sprouts	Raisins
Spelt sprouts	Apricots
Oat groat sprouts	Dried apples
Rolled Oats	Pecans
Buckwheat, sprouted or plain	Walnuts

PREPARE the dough as instructed in the recipe, adding your embellishments during the last few minutes of kneading.

COVER the dough and set to rise for 6–12 hours.

WHEN your dough is ready, divide it into 2 pieces, and press each piece into a pregreased cookie sheet. If you have a pastry roller, you can use this tool to roll the dough evenly and push it to the edge of your sheet. Depending on your preference, make the dough as thin or as thick as you want.

SCORE the dough into pieces as large as you would like to have them (8–12 pieces per sheet is typical), and then cover loosely.

FOR MAXIMUM NUTRITION, NANCY THE HEALTH GURU SAYS:
"All my seeds and grains are either sprouted or at least soaked for eight or more hours. Then they are cooked and completely cooled before I add them to the dough recipe."

LET rise for 2 hours, then bake at 500 degrees for 12 minutes.

WHEN cool, top with grilled veggies and cheese, or slice open to use as a "pocket" bread with meat, cheese, and veggies stuffed inside.

VARIATION

ADD fresh veggies, olive oil, and cheese to the top of your dough right before it goes in the oven for a foccacia-inspired flatbread.

78

Another way to add embellishments to your flatbread is to sprinkle them across the top of dough that has been rolled out into your pregreased baking sheets. You can then press them into the dough with your hands to secure them, or run a pastry roller over the top of the dough a few times.

6

Quick & Easy

P · A · N · C · A · K · E · S, W · A · F · F · L · E · S & C · R · E · P · E · S

MAKES AS MANY AS YOU WANT!

CALEB'S YEAST-ONLY PANCAKES

These are the world's easiest pancakes. They are entirely healthful, fast, simple, and delicious. Don't blink, because they may also be the world's shortest recipe. Here are the ingredients. Or ingredient, I guess I should say:

INGREDIENTS

natural yeast

YEP, that's no typo. That's all there is in this recipe.

JUST grow out some natural yeast, put it in your pan, and fry it up like any other pancake. No need to add any other ingredients.

YOU can make as many or as few pancakes as you want.

THIS recipe is perfect if you have extra starter. And you can also make these pancakes anytime and freeze them for later.

CAUTION: Cook these pancakes on a medium-low temperature—lower than normal pancakes. They cook just a little slower than other pancakes too because if they cook too fast, they will be doughy in the center or will get too dark on the outside. So slow and low is the rule for these one-ingredient pancakes.

82

Oatmeal Natural Yeast Pancakes

INGREDIENTS

1 egg

scant ½ cup milk

1 cup oatmeal (not instant)

2 Tbsp. extra virgin olive oil

¼ tsp. salt

Mixing thoroughly, add:

1 cup natural yeast

COMBINE all ingredients in a bowl.

MIX briefly until combined, taking care not to over-work the batter. (A Danish dough whisk works best.)

POUR batter into heated pan.

SERVE hot.

84

85

Delicious Natural Yeast Pancakes

INGREDIENTS

1 egg

¼ cup milk

3 Tbsp. extra virgin olive oil

¼ tsp. salt

MIXING thoroughly, add:

1 cup natural yeast

(whole wheat, white, or a combination,
    according to preference)

COMBINE all ingredients in a bowl.

MIX briefly until combined, taking care not
to overwork the batter. (A Danish dough whisk
works best.)

FOLD whisked egg white into batter.

POUR into heated waffle iron.

SERVE hot.

87

BANANA BUCKWHEAT PANCAKES

Whenever I make pancakes for breakfast, I make twice what I'll need to feed my family that morning and freeze the leftovers. Then later that same week or the next, I'll defrost them and fry up an egg or two for a five-minute gourmet breakfast. You can even cook smaller pancakes to use in a breakfast sandwich with eggs and a little syrup.

Pastry flour—the flour we get when we grind soft white wheat—works best in pastry-type recipes meant to be light and fluffy. Muffins, cakes, and pancakes all fall in this category. Standard whole wheat will work just fine, but your pancakes will be slightly fluffier with pastry flour.

The baking soda and powder in this recipe is entirely optional. The pancakes will taste equally delicious without these ingredients, but the texture will be markedly different. I use them because at my house, pancakes aren't pancakes without all those light, fluffy bubbles inside that come from the baking soda. Your house may be different, so do what works best for you.

The night before:

INGREDIENTS

1 cup starter

1 cup water

½ cup plain yogurt or kefir

2 cups flour (use pastry flour from soft white wheat if you have it)

¼ cup buckwheat groats (you could substitute rolled oats for this)

MIX ingredients together in a bowl, then cover and set on the counter overnight. Yogurt is a cultured dairy, so it will not spoil.

DID YOU KNOW THAT BUCKWHEAT IS NOT A GRAIN?

IT's actually a fruit seed related to rhubarb and sorrel. The buckwheat in this recipe adds a nutty crunch that compliments the bananas perfectly. For extra crispiness, toast the buckwheat under the broiler in a pan or on a cookie sheet until lightly brown before adding them to the batter. You can also omit them from the batter and toast them to be sprinkled on top as a garnish.

In the morning:

IN a separate bowl, combine using a hand mixer or Danish dough whisk:

INGREDIENTS

1 Tbsp. coconut or olive oil

¼ cup brown sugar (or 1 Tbsp. molasses)

2 eggs

½ cup yogurt or kefir

2 ripe, mashed bananas

1 cup water

ONCE these ingredients are well combined, add them to the starter mixture from the night before.

SPRINKLE:

1 tsp. baking soda,

1 tsp. baking powder

COVER the uncombined mixture and stir (or use a hand mixer) until you have a smooth batter. Do not overmix.

COOK as you would normal pancakes, and eat them hot!

89

CREPES

MAKES APPROXIMATELY 8 CREPES

Crepes are one of my favorite breakfast foods. They are easy to make, delicious, and an excellent way to use up leftover starter. At our house, the tried-and-tested filling of choice is plain yogurt topped with grandma's raspberry jam and peaches from our fall canning. We have literally eaten these for three meals out of the day before, with no regrets, except that we finished off the last of the peaches. All you really need is a blender, some starter, a few odds and ends, and about 15 minutes.

INGREDIENTS

1 cup starter

2 Tbsp. butter (softened)

¼ cup sugar (⅛ cup agave)

¼ tsp. salt

3 eggs

½ tsp. vanilla extract

½ cup milk

½ cup flour

BLEND all the ingredients together in a blender.

POUR into a well-greased frying pan in ¼-cup increments, tilting the pan in a circular movement to spread the batter thin across the bottom.

WHEN bubbles have stopped forming in the batter and the crepe is no longer shiny on top, slide it out of the pan.

TOP with fresh fruit, canned preserves, jam, cream cheese, yogurt, applesauce, or anything else that tickles your fancy!

AIRY, LIGHT, NATURAL YEAST WAFFLES

INGREDIENTS

1 cup starter

2 eggs

1 Tbsp. olive oil

¼ tsp. salt

ADD the yeast mixture into the egg mixture.

USING a spatula (do not use a whisk) gently fold ingredients together until just incorporated.

POUR into waffle iron as usual.

ENJOY!

93

OATMEAL WAFFLES

INGREDIENTS

2 eggs

1 cup regular (not quick cook) rolled oats

¾ cup milk

1 Tbsp. olive oil

¼ tsp. salt

1 cup natural yeast starter

ADD the yeast mixture into the egg mixture.

USING a spatula (do not whisk) gently fold ingredients together until just incorporated.

POUR into waffle iron as usual.

ENJOY!

> *For very picky eaters, add ½ cup milk and ½ cup flour to completely mask any traces of starter flavor.*

94

The Queen of In-Between

I OFTEN FIND MYSELF imagining what my life would be like if I could have everything just the way I wanted it. Three vegetarian meals a day, clean floors, classical music, running and yoga every morning, and endless reading time all top the list.

OF COURSE, if I wanted to run away to another country and start a life of solitude, I could have that life just as I imagine it.

BORING.

AS NICE AS those things all sound, I'll take not-so-vegetarian family meals, dirty socks on the floor, preschool songs, running (after kids) all day, and endless readings of *The Cat in the Hat* with the family I love instead.

I AM A BREAD GEEK, not a bread saint. Yes, I use baking soda, baking powder, brown sugar, and white flour in some of my recipes. I do this for two reasons:

I CANNOT ALWAYS afford to keep the healthier alternatives on hand.

I BAKE TO FEED the psychological expectations of my family as much as to nourish their bodies.

I CREATED MY RECIPES keeping in mind what people most likely have in their kitchen at any given time. For you super-health-food junkies out there, you hardly need me to tell you what substitutions can be made for ingredients listed that don't meet your criteria. Keep to your standards and make the necessary adjustments to the recipes to meet them. If you are an aspiring junkie, check the substitutions list (see page 155) for some ideas to help you get started. Take classes, read some books, and pass useful bread information my way! For those of you who consider the attempt at this form of baking the biggest thing you've ever done for your health, I am so proud of you! Keep it up, and you'll find that you can get addicted to learning new and healthy ways to eat.

WE ALL HAVE to start somewhere, and for me, that somewhere tends to fall in the in-between. Let me give you an example.

IT'S SATURDAY MORNING, and the whole family is begging for pancakes. What happens when I refuse to make the unhealthy white-flour pancakes my husband loves, and my husband refuses to eat my healthy, naturally leavened whole wheat ones? Do we abandon the thought of ever eating breakfast together again? Go our separate ways? Okay, so I'm getting dramatic, but you can see the issue, right? There had to be an in-between. The solution for me was using flour ground from hard white wheat to lighten the color, and adding baking soda to the recipe. The pancakes turned out fluffier (more like his beloved white-flour pancakes) and were less ominous in color and therefore totally edible.

THE SAME WENT for whole wheat, naturally leavened pizza dough. I wouldn't bake the white, and he wouldn't eat the wheat. So I had to settle for very slowly increasing the wheat ratio in my dough over the course of a year or two until my husband was eating whole wheat crusts and didn't even realize it. If I had demanded he eat the way I wanted him to from the get-go, he would have smiled, picked up the phone, and called Domino's. It's a free country. But by being willing to spend some time in the land of in-between (of which I am now Queen), my husband now chooses my pizza over any other. He just needed time to decide to like it on his own.

BREAD GEEK though I am, my first priority in life is not bread—it's people.

BOTH COOKING AND BAKING are acts of kindness, caring, and love. My roasted red bell pepper sourdough artisan bread may not be whole-food healthy, but you should see the smile it puts on my husband's face. For all the whole wheat, naturally leavened goodness he eats without (much) complaining, he deserves a treat from time to time—a treat that tells him that I care enough about his preferences to spend my rare commodities making him happy. And guess what? He is getting way more nutrition from my version than he ever would from the store.

EVERY STEP in the right direction is progress, and the recipes in this book are completely customizable to each and every level of your whole-foods, whole-grain lifestyle. So wherever you are, jump in, amp it up, tone it down, or settle in the in-between so that you and the ones you love can enjoy these recipes together.

97

7

Sweet Things

MUFFINS, CAKES, & CINNAMON ROLLS

SWEET THINGS

WE COULD SIT AROUND ALL DAY AND PRETEND that we are health food purists and that nary an excess of sweet or chocolate has ever passed our lips, but . . . let's face it, we all like to indulge in our own way from time to time.

It is wiser to plan for an indulgent treat that is healthy(er) than to delude yourself into thinking you will never have a moment of weakness again. There will be holidays, family gatherings, and moments of complete alone-ness where all you want is a chocolaty something to make the day melt away. These recipes will help you prepare sweet treats for yourself and your family that have the benefit of properly prepared grains, and enzymes that help your body digest and metabolize sugar.

A NOTE ABOUT PASTRY FLOUR

Like all of our starter recipes, these recipes require setting up a portion of the batter the night before baking, then adding the perishable ingredients the following morning. We use this method to soak your whole wheat flour, increasing available nutrients and reducing harmful enzymes, and to give the start rising power for baking day. **The portion of batter set up the evening before is called a "sponge."**

Muffins, cakes, and other such pastries are on a separate branch of the bread family tree. Bread requires gluten, dough elasticity, and proofing to be successful.

Muffins need none of these. The flour we use for our "sweet things" recipes is called "pastry" flour because it has very little gluten content and can be used in the making of light, airy concoctions, usually of the pastry variety.

Standard bread flour can be substituted for pastry flour in any of these recipes, but the pastries will not rise quite as high or be as airy as with pastry flour. If you grind your own wheat, pastry flour comes from grinding *soft* white wheat. I have used both flours with great success, but I prefer pastry flour.

I had never baked muffins using an overnight grain soak until I tried it for these starter recipes. I think now that I've done it, I'll never go back. Muffins made with the traditional method always came out very thick and a tad bit dry, no matter how much butter or oil I added. I realize now why. As I mentioned in the "Know the Dough" section of this book, whole wheat flour takes longer to absorb moisture than white flour. What I now realize is that 100 percent whole wheat muffins made without a soak of some sort can never be truly moist because the wheat hasn't been given any time to internalize the moisture in the batter. My husband noticed the difference in the first bite of Blueberry Cream muffins. I actually didn't realize how dry my previous muffins had been until he mentioned it. Just another way baking with starts has made my world a tastier place.

101

BLUEBERRY CREAM MUFFINS

These breakfast goodies are a little bit of heaven in a muffin paper. The secret ingredient is sour cream, adding a slightly tangy richness unlike anything you've tasted out of a blueberry muffin. The day I created this recipe, I took one to my mother-in-law (my ultimate taste tester) and crossed my fingers. She took one bite, and another, then looked at me and sighed. "I can tell I'm going to be craving these . . ." Mission accomplished.

SPONGE INGREDIENTS

½ cup starter

1 cup sour cream*

½ tsp. salt

¼ cup brown sugar*

2 cups whole wheat pastry flour

*For healthier muffins, substitute plain yogurt for sour cream, and maple syrup for brown sugar. If you plan to substitute applesauce for the butter, add it to the sponge rather than the morning batter.

MIX the starter into the sour cream with a hand-mixer or Danish dough whisk.

ADD the dry ingredients and combine. This sponge will be a little stiff, quite a bit thicker than muffin batter. Don't worry—the eggs will change that in the final batter.

COVER your bowl with plastic wrap or a damp towel and set out on the countertop overnight (6–12 hours).

For extra fluffy muffins, add 1 teaspoon baking soda to the final batter, before adding blueberries, and fill the muffin tins only ¾ full.

FINAL BATTER INGREDIENTS

½ cup soft butter

¼ cup brown sugar

2 eggs

½ tsp. vanilla

IN a separate bowl, cream together butter and brown sugar. Add eggs and vanilla and mix well.

POUR the mixture into the sponge bowl and mix everything together. The sponge may resist a bit at first, but after a few minutes the texture should be very creamy.

Now to add the blueberries:

IN a separate bowl, gently toss 2 cups blueberries with ½ cup pastry flour. This prevents the blueberries from bleeding their color too much into the batter.

GENTLY fold the blueberries into the batter.

SPOON the batter into a pregreased or lined muffin tin, filling each cup to the top.

STREUSEL TOPPING
(optional, but highly recommended)
½ cup flour
¼ cup brown sugar
3 Tbsp. butter
dash of cinnamon
crushed pecans

MIX the dry ingredients, then use a pastry cutter or
two butter knives to cut the butter into the dry ingredients until you have butter crumbs no larger than peas.
When you have a crumbly streusel topping, spoon it
out onto your muffin batter just before baking.

BAKE the muffins at 350 degrees for 20 minutes,
or until a toothpick inserted into the center comes
out clean.

103

BANANA PECAN MUFFINS

When creating this recipe, I wasn't sure it would be a success. Banana nut muffins tend to have a mild flavor, and I needed to make sure that the flavor of the starter wouldn't be overpowering. I think the key to masking the starter was adding a little buttermilk. The nice thing about this recipe is that not only are you soaking the grains, but the nuts get a good soak too so you get maximum nutritional benefit from everything in the mix. Okay, so I don't know what nutritional "benefits" you get from sugar, but let's say that the emotional benefits more than compensate for lack of nutrition where that's concerned.

SPONGE INGREDIENTS

Combine:

½ cup starter

1 cup buttermilk

½ cup brown sugar

1 tsp. salt

2 cups flour

½ cup crushed pecans*

*I don't love big bites of nut in my muffins, so I use my small food processor to chop the nuts until I have an even mixture of powder and pieces. I'm also not a huge fan of walnuts, but my husband insists they would be perfect in these muffins.

USING a hand mixer or Danish dough whisk, combine the starter and buttermilk. Add the dry ingredients and mix well. If you have made the Blueberry Cream Muffins, please note that this sponge will not be as thick.

COVER and set on the counter overnight.

> FOR *extra fluffy muffins, add 1 teaspoon baking soda to the final batter, and fill the muffin tins only ¾ full.*

FINAL BATTER INGREDIENTS

In a separate bowl cream together:

½ cup butter (room temperature)

¼ cup brown sugar

1 tsp. vanilla

Add:

2 large eggs (one at a time)

2 large, overripe bananas (mashed)

½ tsp. cinnamon

Dash of nutmeg

MIX these wet ingredients well, then pour the mixture into the sponge bowl and mix everything together. The sponge may resist a bit at first, but after a few minutes the texture should be smooth.

GREASE a standard muffin tin, or line with muffin papers.

FILL each cup with ⅓ cup batter, or to the top.

GARNISH muffins with one whole pecan placed in the center of the batter (optional).

PREHEAT oven to 350 degrees and bake 20 minutes, or until toothpick inserted into center comes out clean.

105

MAKES ONE 8-INCH ROUND CAKE

WHOLE WHEAT BLUEBERRY CHOCOLATE CAKE

It seems like every time I introduce a recipe, I make some proclamation about how incredible, unbelievable, and delicious it is. I can't help it. I LOVE these recipes. And only the love that a woman can have for bread and chocolate (otherwise known as cake) can bring the zen I am about to lay on you right now.

This chocolate cake is whole wheat, loaded with anti-oxidants, and has about as much sugar as two bowls of children's breakfast cereal. When we're talking about an entire cake, that's impressive. The very best part is, no one will ever suspect that this cake is good for them. I usually let them get through the first few decadent bites before unloading nutritional information like the side of a cereal box. Some people have trouble lifting a fork to their mouths when they think something healthy is loaded on the other end. You may consider not telling them at all.

SPONGE INGREDIENTS

(The night or morning before):

1 cup starter

1 cup water

2 cups whole wheat pastry flour

6 Tbsp. unsweetened cocoa powder

¼ tsp. salt

POUR water and starter into mixing bowl and stir until starter is dissolved. In a separate small bowl, combine all the dry ingredients. Add the wet ingredients, and mix until everything is evenly moist. The batter will resemble a thick brownie batter.

COVER the bowl with plastic wrap or a damp towel and place on counter for 6–14 hours.

FINAL BATTER INGREDIENTS

2 eggs

2 tsp. vanilla

1½ cup sugar

½ cup fresh or defrosted blueberries

1½ tsp. baking soda

COMBINE eggs, vanilla, sugar, and blueberries in a blender and blend until smooth. Add the soak ingredients and baking soda, blending until combined. If your blender is not particularly powerful, tear the sponge ingredients into chunks as you add it to the blender, making it easier for the blender to combine everything.

PREHEAT oven to 350 degrees. Pour batter into a pregreased 8 x 8 x 2 square pan, or a 9-inch round pan. Bake cake for 30 minutes or until toothpick inserted into center comes out clean.

WARNING: The "fat-free" label stops here. Continue only at your own risk.

MY husband doesn't like chocolate frosting, and his solution is to pour homemade raspberry jam over a slice of hot cake and eat it on the spot. Another delicious fat-free option would be to spread mashed blueberries or sprinkle powdered sugar across the top.

GANACHE FROSTING INGREDIENTS

½ cup semisweet chocolate pieces

1 cup heavy cream

For microwave:

IN a microwave-safe bowl or double-broiler, combine whipped cream and chocolate pieces. For microwave, heat ingredients in one-minute intervals (stirring after each interval) until chocolate melts and mixes evenly into whipped cream. For double-broiler, stir ingredients constantly until ingredients combine evenly.

Stovetop:

HEAT the cream in a small saucepan on medium heat, stirring frequently. Bring it just to a boil (careful not to let it boil over), then remove from heat. Add the chocolate pieces, stirring to melt and incorporate them into the cream. Once the frosting has cooled slightly, pour it onto the cake, spreading from the middle out. Garnish with more fresh blueberries. Eat immediately.

Did you know that cocoa is extremely high in phytic acid? Cocoa that has not been properly soaked contains much more phytic acid than whole wheat flour. Adding the cocoa powder to the "sponge" of this recipe allows the cocoa to soak and neutralize a great deal of the phytic acid that would otherwise be leaching nutrients from your digestive system.

WHOLE WHEAT CINNAMON ROLLS

I have always struggled with whole wheat cinnamon rolls. My mother makes the best cinnamon rolls I have ever tasted, and I have a hard time separating the words "cinnamon roll" from the white fluffiness of those rolls.

The eggs and potato in these rolls compensate immensely for the usual heaviness of whole wheat flour. One of my brothers said, "You can't even tell they're whole wheat!," which I sort of believe, but he is an exceptionally nice guy, so he could have been stroking my ego. Even without the ego boost, these are the best whole wheat cinnamon rolls I have ever had.

The dough is silky smooth and beautiful to work with. I'll admit it was strange to pull the dough out of the bowl after the overnight rise and see little pieces of potato smiling at me. I was worried initially that these rolls were going to turn out like cinnamon hash browns, but the potato disappeared into the crumb completely during baking. Because of the eggs in this dough, I recommend proofing the dough in a cooler place, unlike normal dough, which is proofed at warmer temperatures.

The night before baking

INGREDIENTS

One medium potato (peeled and boiled)

¾ cup buttermilk

½ cup (1 stick) unsalted butter, softened

½ cup dark brown sugar

3 eggs

2 Tbsp. vanilla

½ cup starter

4–5 cups flour

1 tsp. salt

NOTE: *It is very important to follow the order and instructions for this recipe so that the dough will form properly. For reasons I can't explain, this dough turns into a crumbly mess if mixed in the wrong order, and cannot be salvaged.*

BOIL the potato, then mash it with buttermilk until smooth.

IN a separate bowl, use a hand mixer or Danish dough whisk to cream butter and sugar. Add eggs one at a time. Add mashed potato, vanilla, and starter, and mix until well combined.

POUR wet ingredients into bread mixer bowl, then add flour and salt.

KNEAD for 10 minutes, or until the dough can pass the windowpane test. The dough will be soft and somewhat sticky, so don't get carried away with adding extra flour. When in doubt, use the windowpane test (see page 41).

PLACE the dough into a large bowl, cover, and let rise for 6–14 hours.

In the morning

FILLING INGREDIENTS

4 Tbsp. unsalted butter, softened

1¼ cups dark brown sugar

2 Tbsp. ground cinnamon

nuts or raisins for garnish (optional)

GENTLY pull dough from bowl onto your work surface. Divide the dough into two pieces and place one aside, leaving one on the work surface.

> *To speed up this process, substitute cinnamon chips (sold in baking stores and some grocery stores) for butter and cinnamon. Simply pat out the dough, sprinkle cinnamon chips and roll it up!*

ROLL or pat the dough into a rectangle of dough no thinner than ¼ inch.

SPREAD 2 tablespoons of softened butter over the rectangle, leaving a small margin unbuttered along all sides of the dough. Combine your sugar and cinnamon in a small bowl. Sprinkle half of sugar mixture over buttered dough. Try to sprinkle as evenly as possible.

EVERYONE has their own idea of what garnishes the perfect cinnamon roll. For some people, it's raisins. Others prefer walnuts, almonds, or pecans. Whatever your garnish of choice is, now is the time to sprinkle it across the buttered, sugared dough.

STARTING on one of the long sides of the rectangle, roll the dough up into one long tube of dough. Using a sharp knife or unflavored dental floss, slice dough into 1½- to 2-inch cinnamon rolls.

TRANSFER the cut cinnamon rolls into a pregreased 9x13 pan. Cover rolls and let rise for 2 hours (or until dough has doubled) in a warm place.

AFTER the rolls have doubled in size, bake them at 350 degrees for 20 minutes or until rolls are lightly browned. Be careful not to let them get too brown, or they will harden after cooling.

FROSTING INGREDIENTS

3 Tbsp. cream cheese, softened
   (Philadelphia Cream cheese in
      the tub is perfectly soft)

3 Tbsp. milk

1½ cup confectioners sugar

WHILE the rolls are baking, mix up your frosting. After they've cooled slightly but are still warm, pour and spread frosting over the top.

FAQ: *This dough has eggs in it. Will leaving it out on the counter for so long give me salmonella poisoning?*

ANSWER: No.

Salmonella is a bacteria carried on the outside shell of an egg. Whenever you crack an egg open, there is the possibility that some of that bacteria will get into your eggs. Salmonella is killed by cooking, so you have no more danger of salmonella from this dough than you do from cookie dough. Just remember to wash your hands and countertops after handling this dough.

FAQ: *Will the eggs go bad during the long countertop rise?*

ANSWER: **Not likely, and if they did, believe me, you'd know.**

The recipe for this dough originates from a long tradition of egg-doughs that were used far before refrigeration existed. I did a fair amount of asking around among people who use recipes like this on a regular basis, and no one had ever experienced an egg going bad from the long rise. One gentleman commented, "Have you ever *smelled* a rotten egg? Believe me, you'd know if your eggs were bad."

Still a little unsure? Set your dough for the long rise in the refrigerator, but give it a few extra hours to compensate for the cold.

8

ARTISAN BREADS

T·I·P·S & T·E·C·H·N·I·Q·U·E·S FOR S·A·V·O·R·Y S·O·U·R·D·O·U·G·H

SHAPING, DUSTING, STEAMING, AND SLASHING

TECHNICALLY speaking, all the bread in this book is artisan. While the original term *artisan* referred to the baker and not the bread, it has come to refer to any bread made by traditional methods and using long rises. So you, my friend, are an artisan baker every time you bake from this book!

Keeping that in mind, most people have a specific idea in their heads when they think of artisan bread. They tend to picture free-form, slashed loaves with crinkly crusts. I'm going to share with you some of my favorite tricks for making bread that will knock the socks off your guests before they've even taken a bite. The tips below are listed in the order they should be worked into the baking process.

SHAPING

Merely changing the shape of a loaf can increase the "wow" factor. It is easy to shape a loaf into a rounded ball known as a "boule" or into a classic baguette without having to purchase expensive bread forms.

The recipes in this section contain instructions for shaping these artisan breads in boules, but shaping ideas for baguettes, rolls, and sandwich loaves can be found in the shaping tutorials section on page 123.

DUSTING

Cornmeal and flour dusting are both fine details of artisan bread. They are the little hints that equate your bread with expensive French bakery products.

CORNMEAL DUSTING

Lightly dust your baking sheet with cornmeal before placing a rounded boule on it for the final rise. This will not alter the flavor much but will give the finished loaf that extra bit of texture on the bottom most people have come to equate with artisan breads.

FLOUR DUSTING

Before transferring a shaped boule to the cooking sheet, heavily dust your hands and pat the dough all over, leaving flour clinging in spots to the dough. As your bread rises on the pan and in the oven, the flour will "crack," leaving beautiful marks across the

outside of your loaf. You can even go the extra mile and place a decorative leaf or other stencil on top of your dough before dusting, then remove it to leave a pretty shape stenciled in your loaf.

STEAMING

Steaming a loaf during the first 15 minutes of baking is what gives it that signature crackle in the crust. There are plenty of fancy tools available for purchase to do this job, including special misting ovens built specifically for steaming. If you're on a budget like me, you'll just have to make do with what you've got. And guess what? What you've got works just fine.

Preheat the oven to 400 degrees. Fill an oven-safe dish like a pie pan or pyrex dish with hot water (about 2 inches deep) and place it on the bottom rack of your oven. Just before placing it in the oven, very lightly mist the dough with water.

You can do this with a squirt bottle or by flicking water on it with your fingers. Place it in the oven and bake at 400 degrees for 15 minutes (set your timer!), then reduce heat to 350 degrees and bake for another 10–15 minutes.

For extra crackle, you can mist the dough every five minutes with a spray bottle during the first 15 minutes, just make sure not to leave the door open too long each time you mist.

BAD IDEA #1: Filling your steaming dish with only a fine layer of water will result in your pan scorching (metal) or shattering (glass).

BAD IDEA #2: Refilling a glass steaming dish in which the water has boiled down with COLD water will shatter your pan.

FAQ: *I've heard you can spray the sides of your oven to create steam. Does that work?*

ANSWER: Yes, but you probably don't want to.

Unless your oven is spotlessly clean, spraying the sides will produce a dirty steam that makes your bread taste like oven cleaner. Believe me, no amount of butter can cover up that flavor.

SLASHING

Slashing a loaf is an act of pure vanity and great faith. It takes serious guts to take a knife to your precious loaves, but when done boldly and properly, there is nothing so tempting as a well-slashed loaf. The most popular slashes are a single slash down the middle, or two diagonal slashes. Once you become comfortable with slashing, it is easy to imitate slashes on loaves you see in bakeries or on the Internet.

TOOLS

The handiest slashing tool is a very sharp bread knife, one with a large, serrated edge. This is something that most people have lying around the kitchen, even if they don't know it.

My preferred slashing tool is a brand-new razor blade. Not the kind you use for shaving your legs, but the large blade that goes in box-cutters and other garage tools. Razor blades are very sharp and will slash the outer skin of the dough without tugging or wrinkling the loaf. Chances are you have a new one floating around in the garage somewhere at this very moment.

IMPORTANT: Before using it, tie a piece of string or ribbon to your razor blade to prevent it from getting lost in the dough.

METHOD

No guts, no glory. Half-hearted strokes rarely work when it comes to slashing, so don't let fear hold you back. If you want, split one loaf of a two-loaf batch into four smaller boules and practice on those.

Stand over the loaf, feet firmly planted. This makes you feel confident. Hold your slashing tool at a 45-degree angle. Keeping the tool at this angle, slash it through the loaf in one quick, sharp movement, about a ½ inch deep.

It is tempting to hold your slashing tool straight down for slashing, but these slashes tend to fill in as the bread rises, missing out on that great "v" shape you get in a proper slash.

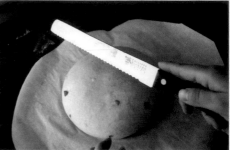
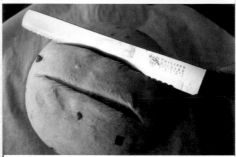
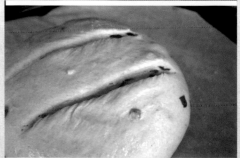

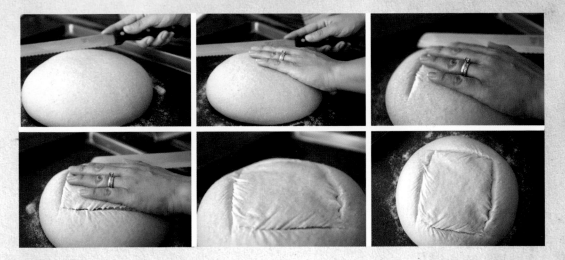

WHEN TO SLASH

Slash your bread immediately before placing it into a hot, steamed oven. Slashing too early (before the oven is preheated) can cause your bread to fall.

THE GOOD NEWS

The good news is all bread, especially artisan bread, looks more professional based on the confidence and flair with which you place it on the table. Slashing didn't work out too well? Loaf looks a little mangled? Call it "rustic sourdough" or "artisan sourdough" and people will think the look is intentional. Or if you're not much of an actor, slice it up and serve it on a pretty platter around some olive oil and a chunk of fresh parmesan. Give 'em the old "razzle dazzle," and they'll never know they're eating your cleverly disguised practice loaf.

A NOTE ABOUT FLOUR IN ARTISAN BREAD

I mentioned earlier that people tend to have preconceived notions about what artisan bread looks like. The same holds true for taste and texture. While a growing number of people appreciate whole wheat artisan bread, the vast majority of folks crave the flavor of white flour in their fancy loaves. When entertaining, or to get on my hubby's good side (he only eats wheat bread because that's all I bake), I use 50/50 or 60/40 white/wheat flour. You are still benefiting from a good percentage of whole wheat flour and a long rise that will make the white flour slightly friendlier to your system. Whole wheat flour baked with a more sour start (I keep a sour start just for artisan bread baking) tends to be very strong in flavor. Not all people like it, even people who love sourdough. This is another reason I don't use 100 percent whole wheat when baking artisan bread for guests. Experiment with ratios that create the best flavor for the people you bake for. Baking is not about bread—it's about people. Let's put some smiles on those people's faces! (They never have to know how much healthiness they're actually eating!)

SAN FRANCISCO SOURDOUGH

This recipe is heavenly and versatile. It is beautiful when garnished with herbs, oils, and cheeses. I never (ever!) bake only one loaf of this bread, for one important reason. Baking two loaves is the only way to make sure you will have a loaf for whatever occasion you are baking for. Without exception in my kitchen, one of the loaves is eaten within thirty minutes of leaving the oven. So if you need a loaf for dinner, or lunch, or a special get-together, baking an additional "decoy loaf" will increase your chances of having something to show for all your hard work.

INGREDIENTS

¼ cup starter

2½ cups water

2 tsp. salt

2 cups whole wheat flour

4½ cups white bread flour

> *I prefer to bake this bread as a rounded boule, so we will shape it that way here. For other options, see the shaping instructions under our recipes for sandwich bread or breadsticks, rolls, and so on. The possibilities really are endless.*

SETTING UP THE DOUGH
(At least 10 hours before baking)

POUR starter, water, and salt into mixer. Turn mixer on just long enough to lightly mix ingredients.

WITH mixer on, add flour 2 cups at a time until dough pulls away from the sides and cleans the bottom half of the mixer bowl. Once dough cleans the bowl, let it knead for 10 minutes, or until the dough can pass the windowpane test (see page 41).

PULL your dough out onto a lightly floured surface and knead 2 or 3 times until dough looks uniform.

LIGHTLY grease a bowl large enough for your dough to double in. Place your dough smooth-side up inside the bowl, and cover with a wet dish towel or greased plastic wrap. Let it rise in a cool place (not the refrigerator) for 6–12 hours.

FEED your starter, and put it in the fridge.

SHAPING

AFTER a minimum of 6 hours, gently turn your dough out of the bowl onto a lightly floured work surface.

PAT lightly to flatten the dough a little and expel any major bubbles. I like this bread just the teeniest bit holey, so I do not use a rolling pin to get out all the bubbles.

PULL the edges of your dough circle toward the center, tucking them as you go. The point is to get all the edges pulled into the middle, like a bundle of dough.

TURN the dough smooth-side up and cup the dough ball gently in your hands. Tip the ball slightly onto its edge and roll it slightly across your work surface, using the tension of the surface to pull the dough tight across the top of the ball. I usually roll in quarter-turn increments, shifting my hands back into starting position after each roll. (For instructional photos on this shaping technique, see page 123.)

FINAL RISE

PLACE the rolled boule smooth-side up onto a pre-greased cookie sheet. I am usually able to put both boules on one sheet if I place them near opposite corners. Spray the tops of the boules with cooking spray and cover with a piece of plastic wrap draped across the top. Let rise for 2 hours, or until doubled in size.

FIFTEEN minutes before your loaves are ready for the oven, fill an oven-safe dish with a few inches of water and place it on the bottom rack of your oven. Preheat your oven to 375 degrees.

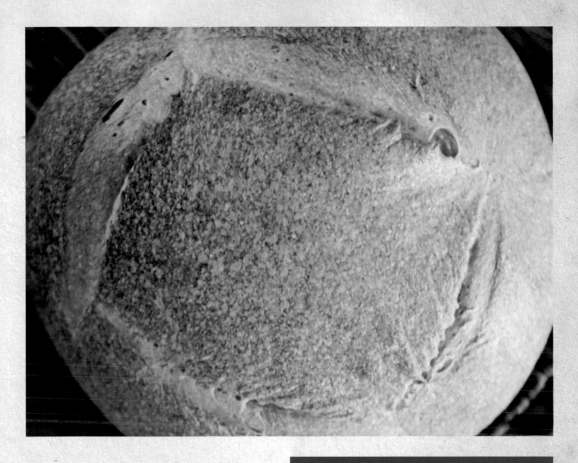

BAKING

IF you plan to slash this loaf, use a razor blade, sharp serrated knife, or other slashing tool to slash your bread once down the center or twice diagonally across your loaf.

PLACE your dough into the preheated oven. Bake for 30 minutes or until a thermometer inserted into the bottom of the boule reads at least 190 degrees.

WHEN your bread is done, set it out to cool on a cooling rack and try really, really hard not to eat both

As a suggestion, I would set the timer for 25 minutes, check the bread to determine how much time is still needed, then reset your timer. Baking times can vary greatly depending on altitude and humidity, so play it safe!

loaves on the spot. If somehow you cannot resist, remember that you baked an extra decoy loaf just for such a weakness. Sit in a sunshiny spot with a heavily buttered slice of steamy bread and let the guilt evaporate!

117

GARLIC ROSEMARY SOURDOUGH

Olive oil adds a moistness to this loaf that will draw you into its fluffiness. My youngest brother (I'm the oldest of six) is thirteen and completely unimpressed with the world at large. He tried so hard to pretend that he didn't care about my dumb bread, but as the loaf began to evaporate amid a frenzy of fingers and mouths, pretense flew out the window. You should have seen the look on his face after he'd eaten a slice and realized there was none left for seconds! The moral of this story is the guilt of eating too much is more bearable than the regret of getting too little.

INGREDIENTS

2½ cups water

¼ cup starter

4 Tbsp. olive oil

½ tsp. crushed garlic (approx. 1 medium clove)

2 Tbsp. coarsely chopped fresh rosemary

2 tsp. salt

2 cups whole wheat flour

4½ cups white bread flour

POUR water, starter, olive oil, garlic, rosemary, and salt into mixer. Turn mixer on just long enough to lightly mix ingredients.

WITH mixer on, add flour 2 cups at a time until dough pulls away from the sides and cleans the bottom half of the mixer bowl. Once dough cleans the bowl, let it knead for 10 minutes, or until the dough can pass the windowpane test (see page 41).

PULL your dough out onto a lightly floured surface and knead 2 or 3 times until dough looks uniform.

LIGHTLY grease a bowl large enough for your dough to double in. Place your dough smooth-side up inside the bowl, and cover with a wet dish towel or greased plastic wrap. Put it to rise in a cool place (not the refrigerator) for 6–24 hours.

FEED your starter, and put it in the fridge.

SHAPING

AFTER a minimum of 6 hours, gently turn your dough out of the bowl onto a lightly floured work surface.

PAT lightly to flatten the dough a little and expel any major bubbles. I like this bread just the teeniest bit holey, so I do not use a rolling pin to get out all the bubbles.

PULL the edges of your dough circle toward the center, tucking them as you go. The point is to get all the edges pulled into the middle, like a bundle of dough.

TURN the dough smooth-side up and cup the dough ball gently in your hands. Tip the ball slightly onto its edge and roll it sideways across your work surface, using the tension of the surface to pull the dough tight across the top of the ball. I usually roll in quarter-turn increments, shifting my hands back into starting position after each roll. (For instructional photos on this shaping technique, see page 123.)

PLACE the rolled boule smooth-side up onto a pregreased cookie sheet. I am usually able to put both boules on one sheet if I place them near opposite corners. Spray the tops of the boules with cooking spray and cover with a piece of plastic wrap draped across the top. Let rise for 2 hours, or until doubled in size.

BAKING

FIFTEEN minutes before your loaves are ready for the oven, fill an oven-safe dish with a few inches of water and place it on the bottom rack of your oven. Preheat your oven to 375 degrees.

IF you are going to slash this loaf, use a razor blade, sharp serrated knife, or other slashing tool to slash your bread once down the center or twice diagonally across your loaf (see page. 114 for slashing techniques).

PLACE your dough into the preheated oven. Bake for 30 minutes or until a thermometer inserted into the bottom of the boule reads at least 190 degrees.

As a suggestion, I would set the timer for 25 minutes, check the bread to determine how much more time is needed, and then reset your timer. Baking times can vary greatly depending on altitude and humidity, so play it safe!

VARIATIONS

THIS dough is excellent shaped into breadsticks, rolls, baguettes, and pizza crusts.

119

ROASTED RED BELL PEPPER AND ASIAGO SOURDOUGH

Let it be known that I am not a great lover of asiago. Well, it's kind of a love-hate thing. I love the way it tastes on a sinfully smothered bagel but hate (hate!) the way it smells while baking.

It was with mild apprehension and a clothespin (nose plug) that I took on my husband's request for an asiago loaf. The Geeklings (my kids) thought it was hilarious to see little cubes popping up under the surface of the dough while we shaped the boules, and I had a hard time keeping their fingers away from them. My daughter actually snuck a little piece of "cheese" from the counter and then came running back with nasty look on her face, begging for a cup of water. Haha! I love "I told you so" moments!

Whatever you do, do not have high hopes for using this bread in a meal or as a gift or any such thing. It will never last that long.

INGREDIENTS

4 Tbsp. olive oil

½ cup diced red bell pepper

4 oz. asiago cheese (cubed)

2½ cups water

¼ cup starter

½ tsp. crushed garlic (approx. 1 medium clove)

2 tsp. salt

3 cups whole wheat flour

3½ cups white bread flour

POUR 1 tablespoon of olive oil into a pan and heat. Add bell pepper and sauté, stirring until bell peppers have softened or begun to brown on the edges. Remove from heat and set aside to cool.

NOW we're going to cube the cheese. Choose your cube size depending on the size of cheese "pockets" you want in your bread. Grating the cheese or chopping it very finely will cause it to melt right into the crumb of the bread. You will be able to taste it, but it will be part of the overall flavor. I recommend a size slightly smaller than standard game dice.

GRATE a small handful of cheese and set it aside for later.

POUR water, starter, remaining olive oil, garlic, and salt into mixer. Turn mixer on just long enough to lightly mix ingredients. Add bell pepper and oil from pan.

WITH mixer on, add flour 2 cups at a time until dough pulls away from the sides and cleans the bottom half of the mixer bowl. Once dough cleans the bowl, let it knead for 10 minutes, or until the dough can pass the windowpane test (see page 41).

PULL your dough out onto a lightly floured surface and knead 2 or 3 times until dough looks uniform.

LIGHTLY grease a bowl large enough for your dough to double in. Place your dough smooth-side up inside the bowl and cover with a wet dish towel or greased plastic wrap. Put it to rise in a cool place (not the refrigerator) for 6–24 hours.

FEED your start, and put it in the fridge.

SHAPING

AFTER a minimum of 6 hours, gently turn your dough out of the bowl onto a lightly floured work surface.

PAT lightly to flatten the dough a little and expel any major bubbles. I like this bread just the teeniest bit holey, so I do not use a rolling pin to get out all the bubbles.

120

Some people prefer to knead the cheese into the loaf the next day right before shaping, but I like putting it in before the long rise the night before. Sometimes the cubes are hard to knead in without losing all the beautiful bubbles you've developed in your loaf, and I think the cheese flavors the dough so nicely when it's had a chance to sit overnight.

PULL the edges of your dough circle toward the center, tucking them as you go. The point is to get all the edges pulled into the middle, like a bundle of dough.

TURN the dough smooth-side up and cup the dough ball gently in your hands. Tip the ball slightly onto its edge and roll it sideways across your work surface, using the tension of the surface to pull the dough tight across the top of the ball. I usually roll in quarter-turn increments, shifting my hands back into starting position after each roll. (For instructional photos on this shaping technique, see page 123.)

PLACE the rolled boule smooth-side up onto a pregreased cookie sheet. I am usually able to put both boules on one sheet if I place them near opposite corners. Spray the tops of the boules with cooking spray and cover with a piece of plastic wrap draped across the top. Let rise for 2 hours, or until doubled in size.

BAKING

FIFTEEN minutes before your loaves are ready for the oven, fill an oven-safe dish with a few inches of water and place it on the bottom rack of your oven. Preheat your oven to 375 degrees.

IF you are going to slash this loaf, use a razor blade, sharp serrated knife, or other slashing tool to slash your bread once down the center or twice diagonally across your loaf (see page 114 for slashing techniques).

PLACE your dough into the preheated oven. Bake for 30 minutes or until a thermometer inserted into the bottom of the boule reads at least 190 degrees.

AS a suggestion, I would set the timer for 25 minutes, check the bread to determine how much more time is needed, and then reset your timer. Baking times can vary greatly depending on altitude and humidity, so play it safe!

WHEN the dough is ready to come out of the oven, sprinkle it with the cheese we grated earlier and stick it back in for a minute or two to melt and slightly brown the cheese. Remove, cool (yeah right!), and eat!

121

9

SHAPING
TUTORIALS

SHAPING TUTORIALS

THE WAY YOU SHAPE YOUR **BREAD** can determine not just the way it looks, but also the way it bakes and tastes. Texture is a huge part of the way we perceive the taste of a bread, and shaping plays a big part in the texture of a finished loaf. Here are a few basic shaping tutorials to get you started.

SANDWICH LOAVES

LIGHTLY pat the dough out to form a rectangle, leaving the dough about ½ inch thick. Working with the long sides of the rectangle, fold the dough in thirds, like you would a fancy bath towel. You should now have a long rectangle ⅓ as wide as the original rectangle.

NOW fold the dough in thirds again, using the ends this time. You now have a tight packet of dough.

TURN the dough over so it is smooth-side up and place it in your pregreased sandwich loaf pan. Lightly press the dough to flatten it slightly and help it fill the bottom of the pan.

COVER and let rise for 2 hours.

BOULES

LIGHTLY pat the dough out to form a circle. Artisan bread tends to have more holes in it, so leave lots of bubbles.

PULL the edges of your dough circle toward the center, tucking them as you go. The point is to get all the edges pulled into the middle, like a bundle of dough.

TURN the dough bundle smooth-side up and cup the dough ball gently in your hands. Tip the ball slightly onto its edge and roll it slightly across your work surface, using the tension of the surface to pull the dough tight across the top of the ball. I usually roll in quarter-turn increments, shifting my hands back into starting position after each roll.

ONCE your ball of dough has a tight, even surface, place it smooth-side up on a pregreased baking sheet. Cover with a large bowl or greased piece of plastic wrap and let rise for 2 hours.

CALEB WARNOCK & MELISSA RICHARDSON

BAGUETTES

Baguettes can be any length or width, depending on what you are baking your bread for and how long your baking sheet is. One loaf of dough will make one nice-looking, average-sized baguette.

FLATTEN your dough out gently to form a rectangle about ½ inch thick. Take the edge of one long side of the rectangle and fold it into the center of the rectangle, pressing down to seal the edge into the middle of the dough. Do the same with the opposite side, again using your fingers or the heel of your hand to seal the edge of the dough into the center. tech

REPEAT.

WHAT this process does is gently tighten the "skin" of the dough to help it hold its shape during baking.

TAKE your sealed dough and, starting with both hands in the middle, begin to roll it back and forth to work the dough out into a "snake" an inch or two shorter than the length of your baking sheet. Once you have reached the right length, tuck the ends under and seal them off.

GENEROUSLY flour a towel that can accommodate the length of your dough. Place it on a countertop where it will be undisturbed during rising. Place your baguette on the towel and wrinkle the towel before and after the baguette, forming 2 protective towel bumps just barely taller than the height of your dough.

WHEN your next baguette is formed, place it alongside the protective bump behind the first baguette, and form another after it. Continue this process until you have formed all the baguettes you will be baking. You should see hills of towel and valleys of dough.

LET rise for 2 hours, then bake for 20 minutes at 375 degrees following the instructions for steaming on page 113.

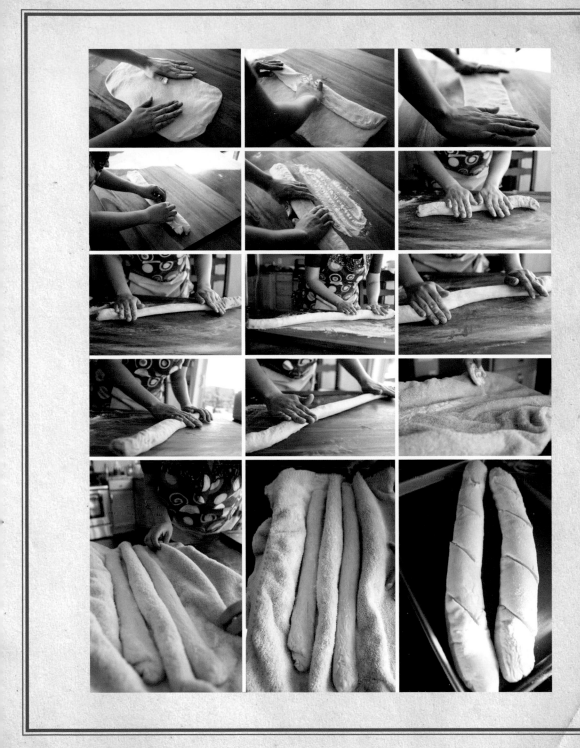

131

ROLLS

For each of these recipes, you will need to choose a dough from the Basic Six or an artisan bread recipe and prepare the dough following those instructions until it is ready for shaping.

ONCE the dough is ready for shaping, find the roll type you would like to use and follow the instructions for those rolls to the end.

REMEMBER that our recipes are measured for 2 loaves of dough. If you need only a small number of rolls, here are some suggestions:

USE one loaf for rolls, the other for a loaf of bread.

MAKE both loaves into rolls, bake them, then freeze what you will not be using right away.

GIVE some away to someone who needs a smile! (I am a serial bread-gifter.)

HALF the recipe and mix the dough by hand.

DOUGH SUGGESTION:

These rolls can be made using any of the dough recipes. They are delicious wheat or white, savory or sweet. I have noticed in my baking that people tend to expect a slightly sweeter dough for dinner rolls, so my tendency is to use the dough from the Honey Molasses Loaf recipe (page 56).

DON'T FORGET TO WASH YOUR ROLLS!

Yep, you heard me. Rolls look especially beautiful with an egg, milk, or butter wash. Here's how to know which wash is right for you.

WHOLE EGG WASH
Mix one whole egg with a tablespoon of water. Brush this gently over the top of the roll right before baking. This will give the rolls a shiny, bronzed surface.

EGG WHITE WASH
For 1 egg white, use 2 teaspoons of water. This will give you a clear-coat wash. The same shiny-ness, no golden tan—like how you look when you put on sunscreen after a long winter.

EGG YOLK WASH
Mix 2 teaspoons of water for each egg yolk you use. This makes a very golden crust.
CAUTION: *Too much egg wash or not using enough water in your wash will cause the egg itself to cook up during baking, leaving little scrambled eggs in your nooks and crannies where the wash pooled after application.*

MILK WASH
Milk will bronze your crust, just like egg, but will be slightly softer and not quite as shiny.

BUTTER
Brush a little bit of melted butter onto your rolls before or after baking to make a soft, flavorful crust.

WATER WASH
I don't recommend water washes for rolls. Water washes help create a crispy crust, but for rolls, it is hard to do just right without making too much crust for an enjoyable roll.

133

CRESCENT ROLLS

INGREDIENTS

Dough that has been prepared and
   proofed 6–24 hours

Pizza cutter or dough scraper

Melted butter for brushing over dough

Pastry brush (optional)

Cookie sheets

PREPARE dough for two loaves using the recipe of your choice.

SEPARATE the dough into 2 equal pieces.

TAKE a section of the dough and, using a rolling pin, roll the dough out into a circle of dough ¼ inch thick.

PREHEAT your oven to 350 degrees.

USING a pizza cutter or dough scraper, cut the dough like a pizza until you have 16 equal "wedges."

USING the pastry brush or your fingers, brush your dough with a generous amount of melted butter.

ROLL each wedge, starting at the fatter end and rolling toward the point.

PLACE each roll onto a pregreased cookie sheet in a crescent shape, with the tip beneath the roll.

COVER and let rise for 1–2 hours, or until doubled in size.

BAKE in oven at 350 degrees for 15–20 minutes or until the bottoms of the rolls are lightly browned.

BRUSH hot rolls with butter and serve.

GARNISHES

DEPENDING on the meal you are serving, small embellishments can be added to these rolls to cater to the flavor of your dish. These garnishes can be sprinkled or spread across the tops of the buttered

wedges before they are rolled. Here are some you might consider:

Garlic salt

Parmesan cheese

Mozarella cheese

Any cheese! Rosemary Italian seasoning

Craisins

Honey

Sesame seeds

THE ¼-inch thickness is important for a number of reasons. With whole wheat dough, having thicker dough will lead to baked rolls that are almost mini-loaves in themselves. Whole wheat bread will always be more dense than white. I made the mistake of leaving the dough too thick for Thanksgiving rolls one year. The rolls themselves were delicious, but no one got through an entire roll, they were that filling. So roll with caution. Dough that is too thick will overfill a belly; dough that is too thin will lack sufficient rising power.

CLOVERLEAF ROLLS

I don't know why, but these rolls remind me of Thanksgiving. I love to make these for the holidays, I think they look so pretty on the table. They are especially nice with a milk or butter wash.

DIVIDE each loaf of dough into 36 pieces.

SHAPE each piece into a ball, pulling the edges into the middle underneath to make a smooth top.

PLACE 3 balls in each greased muffin cup, smooth-sides up.

COVER and let rise for 2 hours.

BAKE at 350 degrees for 12–15 minutes, or until done.

136

137

WHIMSY ROLLS

DIVIDE each loaf of dough into 24 pieces.

ROLL each piece out into a dough "snake" about 9 inches long.

STARTING at one end, and leaving the dough on the countertop, begin to roll the dough up along itself until all the dough is used and you have a spiral that looks like a cinnamon roll.

TUCK the free end under the rolled dough.

PLACE the roll in a greased muffin tin and repeat the process with the rest of the dough.

COVER and let rise for 2 hours.

BAKE at 350 degrees for 12–15 minutes, or until done.

139

ROSETTES

This is not really a roll, but could be. I love using this shaping technique for hamburger buns (sprinkled with sesame seeds) or for making any old sandwich look like it came from a deli.

FOR sandwich-sized buns, divide each loaf of dough into 16 pieces. For smaller rosette rolls, divide each load of dough into 24 pieces.

ON a lightly oiled surface, roll each piece into a 12-inch-long rope.

TIE dough into a loose knot, leaving 2 long ends sticking out either side. Tuck top end under roll.

BRING bottom end up and tuck into center of roll. Pinch loose ends together.

PLACE 2–3 inches apart on greased baking sheet. Flatten slightly with palm of hand if making hamburger buns.

COVER and let rise for 2 hours, then bake at 350 degrees for 12–15 minutes, or until done.

142

10 BONUS RECIPES

S·C·O·N·E·S, B·R·E·A·D·S·T·I·C·K·S, & P·I·Z·Z·A D·O·U·G·H

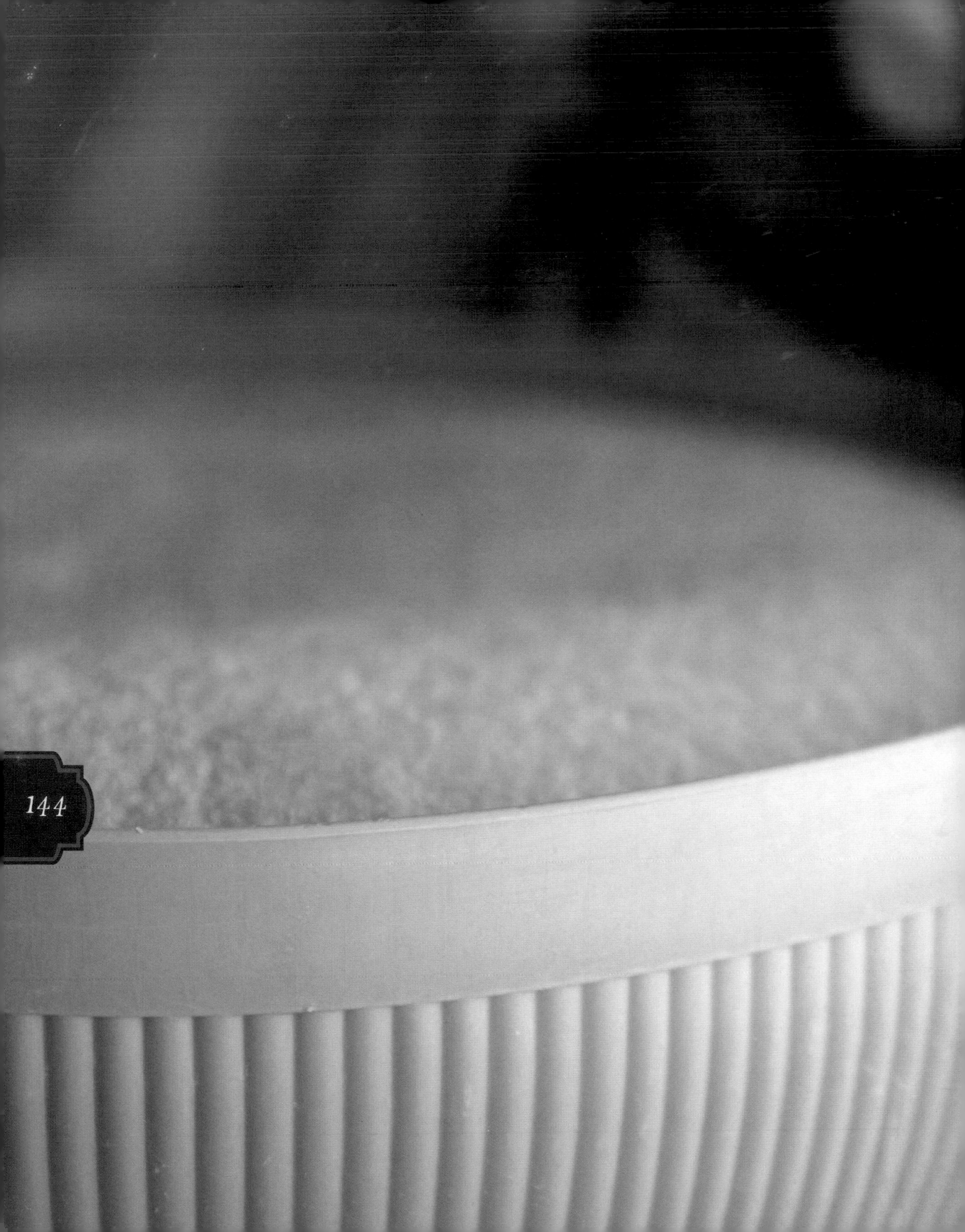

BONUS RECIPES

THERE ARE ENDLESS ways to use these bread recipes to enhance the nutrition of your breakfast, lunch, or dinner. Here are a few quick and easy ideas for ways to do just that using any of the recipes in this cookbook, and a few delicious extras for what to do with loaves that don't turn out.

NOTE: These recipes can be made using dough from any recipe found in the Basic Six or Artisan Breads section, although for the scones you may want to use a sweeter dough. The dough should have had its long rise and be ready for shaping. For the bread machine recipe, simply use the dough setting rather than the bread baking setting.

SCONES

HEAT oil in a deep pan. (I use olive oil, which smokes a bit more than other oils but is healthier). Cutting off pieces of dough, form scones by hand. Fry until golden brown on both sides and serve.

BREAD MACHINE SCONES: When the machine is done preparing the dough, allow dough to rise until doubled in size, about 2 hours, then continue with directions above.

BREADSTICKS

(MAKES 2 cookie sheets of breadsticks; for one cookie sheet, halve the ingredients of the original recipe or use the extra dough to make something else.)

DIVIDE dough in half and roll out to fill two cookie sheets (use a cookie sheet with raised edges). Allow dough to rise in cookie sheets until doubled in size, about 90 minutes. Pour ¾ cube melted butter evenly over the dough.

SPREAD the melted butter with a spatula if necessary to cover the entire surface of the dough. Using a pizza cutter, and without removing dough from cookie sheet, run the cutter up and down to cut dough into strips. Sprinkle 1 cup grated parmesan cheese over the cut strips.

BAKE in a 350-degree oven for 10–13 minutes, until dough just barely begins to brown. Remove and serve.

147

PIZZA DOUGH

MAKES 2 REGULAR CRUST PIZZAS
OR 4 THIN-CRUST PIZZAS

THE important thing to know about this recipe is that while it takes only 3 minutes to prepare, you will need to start the dough in the morning to have the dough ready for pizza at dinnertime.

DIVIDE dough into 2 or 4 equal balls. Roll out each ball and place on pizza trays. Top with desired sauce and toppings. Bake in oven at 375 degrees for 10–12 minutes.

FOR BREAD MACHINE PIZZA CRUSTS:

When the machine completes the dough setting, simply leave the dough inside the machine to rise for the rest of the day. When you are ready to make dinner, the dough will be at its full raise inside the machine. Remove and roll out for pizza.

CALEB WARNOCK & MELISSA RICHARDSON

TWO WAYS TO EAT A BRICK

A "BRICK" in bread terms is what you get when, after all your hard work, the loaf that comes out of the oven could be used as an edible paper weight.

Bricks are more common among bakers of whole wheat bread and even more common among natural yeast-ers. Think about it, you are baking your bread with something living, organisms that contribute to the fundamentals of our ability to be alive at all. If there is one thing we all know about life, it is that where there are living things, there are variables. Your start may have a slump, your your proofing area may be too cold or too warm, or a butterfly could flap its wings in Africa, upset the balance of the universe, and flatten your bread simultaneously.

It's not just the microscopic living variables that can create a brick either. I have had beautifully risen loaves deflated by little fingers looking for a doughy snack. One morning I had just uncovered the loaves about to go into the oven when my husband walked in the kitchen. He looked at the plump dough on the counter and then inexplicably lifted a hand and gave the dough a smart "smack!" across the top. It made a funny sound, and he and the kids laughed, . . . until the loaf collapsed in the pan. The three of them looked at me with wide eyes, and my husband said (very apologetically), "Was that loaf important?" Luckily, it wasn't, but I then had yet another brick on my hands.

Needless to say, I have a lot of experience with using up the occasional brick. Of course, you can always feed the ducks or the birds at the park, but there are other, tastier options as well.

BREAD CRUMBS

Bread crumbs are one of my most common ways to use up a brick. It doesn't take much preparation, they store for a very long time, and can be used in so many non-bread recipes.

STEP 4: TOAST AGAIN

IF your crumbs are absolutely dry, you can skip this part, but if there is any doubt, another toast can prevent molding. Pour your crumbs onto the cookie sheet and put them back into the oven for another brief toasting. Stir the crumbs a few times to make sure they are done evenly.

STEP 5: LABEL AND STORE

POUR your crumbs into the storage container of your choice, labeling it with the date and contents. I have never had bread crumbs in my pantry longer than a few months without using them, so I am not sure for how long they stay good. My suggestion is to follow your nose. When wheat bread molds, there is no missing that smell, so if it smells fresh, it probably is.

STEP 1: SLICE

SLICE your brick into very thin slices, keeping each slice as evenly thick as possible.

STEP 2: TOAST

PLACE as many slices as you can fit onto a cookie sheet and place them in the oven at about 350 degrees. Set the timer for 3 minutes so you remember to check them before they burn. Flip the slices over, toasting both sides until the slices are *completely* dry. Moist bread crumbs will mold.

STEP 3: CRUMBLE

BREAK up the slices into smaller pieces and place them in a food processor. Pulse the motor until you have the consistency of crumbs you prefer. If you don't have a food processor, you can crumble them by hand, with a mortar and pestle, or with a bowl and the back of a measuring cup.

BREAD CRUMBS AS TOPPINGS

Bread crumb toppings need to be particularly crisp to lend just the right effect to a dish. We accomplish this by tossing our seasoned bread crumbs in a small amount of melted butter or oil. 1 tablespoon per 2 cups of bread crumbs is usually a good standby. LAUREL'S KITCHEN BREAD BOOK suggests sautéing your bread-crumbs in butter with onion until crisp for toppings. While I've never tried it myself, that woman is right about just about everything.

150

STEP 6: USING YOUR CRUMBS

I use my crumbs in many recipes like meat loaf, breaded chicken, and breaded pork chops and as a topping for vegetable dishes. For recipes with a strong flavor, I use plain crumbs. Sometimes you want your crumbs to have their own distinct flavor. In that case, here are a few tips for preparing your crumbs to use in recipes.

SEASONING

Put your measured bread crumbs into a bowl and sprinkle in dashes of any seasonings that would complement your dish.

For ITALIAN DISHES like Breaded Eggplant Parmesan or stuffed pasta, a standard Italian seasoning mix sprinkled into the crumbs is easy and adds just the right flavor.

POULTRY or PORK DISHES are complemented well by sage, thyme, rosemary, garlic, and onion salt or powder, pepper, or even a slight dash of red pepper.

BEEF ENTREÉS are complemented well by McCormick's Hamburger seasoning or any other steak or beef seasoning. If you don't have any of these, onion salt and pepper alone can taste great.

FISH is paired well with dill, lemon pepper, lemon thyme, garlic, and salt and pepper.

151

BREAKFAST SOUFFLÉ

One of the many wonderful things I married into when I said "I do" to my husband was the recipe for his mother's Breakfast Soufflé. The original recipe calls for standard white bread, but when I tried it using one of my whole wheat bricks, we both agreed the flavor was even better than before, which neither of us thought possible. Both of these recipes require time for the bread to absorb the eggs and milk and therefore require a long refrigeration before baking and a long, low temperature bake.

The night before:

INGREDIENTS

8 slices bread, crust trimmed and cubed

2 cups cheese, diced or shredded

2½ cups milk

4 eggs slightly beaten

¾ tsp. dry mustard

PLACE bread in bottom of oblong glass baking dish. Place cheese evenly on top.

MIX wet ingredients and pour evenly over bread and cheese. Cover, and let stand overnight in refrigerator.

In the morning (2 hours before serving):

INGREDIENTS

1½ lbs. sausage, browned

1 (10.75-oz.) can cream of mushroom soup

½ cup milk

BEFORE baking, brown sausage, and dice and sprinkle across the top. Mix soup and milk and pour over soufflé.

BAKE uncovered at 275 degrees for 1½ hours or until center is set. Serve immediately.

APPENDIX

SUBSTITUTIONS

BROWN SUGAR

Sucanat can be substituted for brown sugar measure for measure. Sucanat is essentially dried cane juice, prior to molasses extraction, and still houses the plant's vitamins and minerals. Oftentimes for muffins I will substitute **maple syrup** for brown sugar, measure for measure.

BUTTER

For vegan or lactose intolerant bakers, I recommend **Earth Balance** spread in place of butter. Earth Balance can be substituted measure for measure. It is a healthier alternative that will still give you that butter flavor. Do not confuse Earth Balance with Smart Balance, which is margarine and very unhealthy.

Soy Lecithin can be substituted measure for measure in place of butter. Lecithin has a long list of health benefits, including being a fat emulsifier, but is also an isolated substance (see the section on dough enhancers on page 44). While it is FDA approved, I do not recommend it for daily, long-term use. WARNING: Lecithin is extremely difficult to wash out of measuring cups. I never measure my lecithin. Usually I will place the spoon size I need next to the mixing bowl, and pour lecithin into the dough until I feel like it would have filled the spoon I am looking at. It's rudimentary, but it works.

Applesauce can also be substituted measure for measure, but I only recommend this for the muffin recipes.

BUTTERMILK

If you're out of buttermilk, measure out the same amount of **regular milk, then add one tablespoon of vinegar or lemon juice per cup of milk.** Stir the vinegar or lemon juice into the milk, then allow it to stand five minutes before using. It is also possible to substitute **plain yogurt** or **kefir** for buttermilk. For those who are lactose intolerant, the same method can be used with *plain* (not vanilla) **soy** or **rice milk**.

EGGS

Use **1 tablespoon ground flax seed mixed with 1½ tablespoon of water,** per egg.

MOLASSES

As far as flavor is concerned, there is no substitute for molasses. If, however, you don't happen to have any on hand or you have a rare psychological blockage to the mere idea of molasses, **brown sugar** or **honey** can be used instead.

MILK

Any recipe in this cookbook that calls for milk can be made using **soy, rice,** or **almond milk**. In some cases, water can be used as a substitute, but it may affect the flavor or texture of the recipe. I prefer to substitute almond milk in my sweetbread baking. I love the richness and creaminess it adds to the bread.

OLIVE OIL

I do not recommend substituting the olive oil in the artisan breads. These breads were formulated for flavor, and the olive oil is a key ingredient to the overall flavor of the loaves. For non-savory loaves, **coconut oil** or **butter** can be easily substituted.

PASTRY FLOUR

Any of our recipes that call for pastry flour can also be made using **standard whole wheat baking flour**. You cannot, however, use pastry flour in a recipe that does not call for it. Pastry flour is what you get when you grind soft white wheat. It has less gluten and, when used in baking, can produce lighter, fluffier results than flour ground from hard white or hard red wheat. It does not have enough gluten to raise a loaf of standard bread.

SOUR CREAM

Plain yogurt can be substituted cup for cup. I never use sour cream in my cooking because plain yogurt will give you the same flavor and texture without the fat. For maximum healthiness, use a yogurt with lots of probiotic cultures. My favorites are Mountain High and Brown Cow.

FAVORITE PRODUCTS

BOSCH MIXER

I love my Bosch. *Love.* I have put my machine through some serious workouts, and it has risen to the occasion every time. The only time I used a different brand of mixer for bread making, I ended up in a smoking heap like the crazy chef from the Muppets. Dough was climbing the hook, the machine was dancing all over the countertop, and after a few minutes, the whole thing started to smoke. The disaster may or may not have been the machine's fault, but any appliance that can't handle basic levels of human inexperience and stupidity does not belong in my kitchen. For me, Bosch stands for Brilliantly Optimized for Stupid Cooking Humans. In other words, it was made just for me.

BREAD BAGS

I use bread bags to store my bread in. I could probably find a more "environmentally friendly" option, but for now, this works for me. It  is also nice to have bread bags in the house when I want to gift some bread to a friend or neighbor.

COOLING RACK

Using a cooling rack for your bread will prevent your bread from getting damp and gummy underneath while it cools on the counter. You never want to put damp bread into a bag or container, and cooling racks take care of that problem.

CREPE MAKER

Honestly, when I got my crepe maker as a Christmas present ten years ago, my thought was "When in the world am I ever going to use *this*?" And really, it wasn't until I started cooking regularly with my starter that the answer to that question turned from "never" to "weekly." With my crepe maker, I never burn crepes, don't have to wash extra pans, and don't have to hover over the stove. I simply pour batter from my blender into a pie pan, dip the nonstick surface in batter, set it on the counter, and wait for the little red light to come on. Ding! This way I can cook crepes while I prepare the fillings, set the table, and coax children from their beds.

DANISH DOUGH WHISK

These whisks are every bit as fantastic as their funky shape implies. It is wonderful at mixing up batters and no-knead dough. In fact, my hand mixer broke three years ago, and I never bought a new one, because everything I needed to make with it could be either put in the blender or handled by my Danish dough whisk.

MAGIC BULLET

This little wonder-of-an-appliance gets used in my baking all the time. It is compact, quick to get out, quick to put away, and easy to clean up after. In one minute flat I can have coarsely ground flax seed, oatmeal, or pecans using this appliance. It will not do the job of large food processors, but it can handle small, quick jobs like nothing else I've used.

DOUGH SCRAPER

I keep two scrapers in my kitchen. One is a sturdy plastic variety with an easy-to-grip handle, and the other is a soft plastic scraper also traditionally used in cake decorating. The sturdier scraper I use for dividing dough into smaller loaves or rolls, cleaning work surfaces with dried dough on them, and to help lift sticky dough off the work surface. I use my soft scraper for gently teasing dough out of bowls (it can easily conform to the shape of the bowl) and as an aid in kneading sticky doughs.

MASON JARS

By "mason" jars, I mean glass canning jars of any brand. That's just what we call them around our house. Mason jars have long been my standby when it comes to starter storage containers. They come in such a wide variety of sizes and can fill so many uses. Unlike modern plastics and some metals, they will not leach dangerous chemicals into your food and, while breakable, will last almost forever. Wide-mouth quart jars are best for starter storage, wide or narrow-neck can be used for sprouting, and the smaller jam jars are excellent for keeping a very small quantity of starter or gifting starter to friends.

NUTRIMILL GRINDER

Really, my grinder is my best friend. Mixers usually get all the glory, but the grinders are the unsung heroes of bread making. I would  never have come this far in baking if not for the financial flexibility of my grinder. My bread is cheaper and tastier and never depends on a trip to the store. As you know (or will soon find out), I am a Bosch girl, so my grinder of choice is the Nutrimill. There are hundreds of options for grinders, so if the Nutrimill is not for you, do a little research and you are sure to find one that is. The website www.breadtopia.com is a great resource for grinder information.

PASTRY ROLLER

Pastry or pizza rollers are small, versatile, and easy to store. I love being able to roll dough out right in the pan for pizzas and flatbreads or shape rolls without having to wrangle a huge rolling pin. For years I lived in apartments with no space for using or storing a rolling pin, and this little pastry roller really came to the rescue.

PLASTIC CANNING JAR LIDS

Most health food stores now carry a variety of plastic canning jar lids. Some have holes to use for sprouting, others are solid. If you are keeping your starter in a canning jar, a plastic lid can be helpful. It will not create an airtight seal (your starter needs to breathe a little) and is easy to throw in the dishwasher for cleaning.

RUBBER BANDS

I found out the magical use of rubber bands in baking by accident. I was using a blue rubber band to identify which starter was Gale (I had put them in identical jars) when I realized that I could also use rubber bands to help me measure whether or not my starter is doubling in volume. I simply place the rubber band at the level of the starter in the jar right after feeding, then check back in 24 hours to see how high above the rubber band my starter has grown.

THERMOMETER

There are about a thousand different brands of kitchen thermometers out there, some of them very expensive. I think I bought mine at the grocery store for a few bucks. You don't need anything fancy or digital,  just a little thermometer that can be poked in the bottom of a loaf. For many years I had a tendency to under-bake or burn my bread, and using a thermometer was the only sure way to bake.

BIBLIOGRAPHY

Carr-Elsing, Debra. "Friendship and Bread in the Style of Pioneers." *The Capital Times*, 2001. HighBeam Research, 20 Dec. 2010, www.highbeam.com.

Cobb, Allan B. "Genetically Engineered Foods." *Animal Sciences*. The Gale Group, 2002. HighBeam Research, 21 Dec. 2010, www.highbeam.com.

Cohen, M. "Société Industrielle Lesaffre." *International Directory of Company Histories*. Thomson Gale, 2007. HighBeam Research, 24 Dec. 2010, www.highbeam.com.

Eades, Michael R. "Heartburn Cured." *The Blog of Michael R. Eades, M.D.* (blog). www.proteinpower .com/drmike/archives/2005/11/Heartburn_Cured.html. Accessed Jan. 18, 2011.

"Eat Whole Grains." LiveStrong.com. www.livestrong. com/article/93519-acid-reflux-remedies/#ixzz19BgvtO8s. Accessed Jan. 1 2011.

"First Step to Controlling Acid Reflux with a Home Remedy." EzineArticles.com. www.ezinearticles.com/? The-First-Step-to-Controlling-Acid-Reflux-With-a-Home-Remedy&id=3988237. Accessed Jan. 1, 2011.

Gantz, Rachel. "Iogen First Licensed Customer of Genetically-Altered Yeast." Renewable Fuel News. Hart Energy Publishing, 2004. HighBeam Research, 21 Dec. 2010, www.highbeam.com.

Gullick, Roberta C. "Grab Some Yeast from a Juniper Berry." *Countryside & Small Stock Journal*. Countryside Publications, 2002. HighBeam Research, 21 Dec. 2010, www.highbeam.com.

"Harvard Public Health Review 2000." Harvard School of Public Health. Nutrition Source website: www.hsph .harvard.edu/review/review_2000/featureaging.html. Accessed Jan. 1, 2011.

Hassan, Yousef and Lloyd B. Bullerman. "Antifungal Activity of Lactobacillus paracasei ssp. Tolerans Isolated from a Sourdough Bread Culture." *International Journal of Food Microbiology* 121, no. 1 (Jan. 2008): 112–15.

"Health Gains from Whole Grains." Harvard School of Public Health. Nutrition Source website: www.hsph. harvard.edu/nutritionsource/what-should-you-eat /health-gains-from-whole-grains.

"Heartburn Drugs Linked to Pneumonia Risk," WebMD Health News. www.webmd.com/heartburn-gerd/news/ 20101219/heartburn-drugs-linked-to-pneumonia-risk. Accesssed Jan. 1, 2011.

Hughes, Kerry. "A Day Off: Use Origin-Based Sourdoughs." Prepared Foods. BNP Media. HighBeam Research, 20 Dec. 2010, www.highbeam.com.

"Infections, Fractures Linked to Acid Reflux Drugs." WebMD Health News. www.webmd.com/heartburn-gerd /news/20100510/c-diff-infections-fractures-linked -to-acid-reflux-drugs. Accessed Jan. 1 2011.

Katina, K., et al. "Potential of Lactic Acid Bacteria to Inhibit Rope Spoilage in Wheat Sourdough Bread." *LWT Food Science & Technology* 35, no. 1 (Feb. 2002): 38.

Kopsahelis N., et al. *Bioresource Technology* 100, no. 20 (Oct. 2009): 4854–62. Date of Electronic Publication: 2009 Jun 10.

Lopez, H. W., et al. "Making Bread with Sourdough Improves Mineral Bioavailability from Reconstituted Whole Wheat Flour in Rats." *Nutrition* 19, no. 6 (June 2003): 524–30.

McLaughlin, Katy. "Was That Blob in Your Kitchen Born in the Gold Rush?" *Wall Street Journal.* May 3, 2010.

"Meal Planning Tips Prevent Heartburn." WebMD Health News. www.webmd.com/heartburn-gerd/guide/11-meal-planning-tips-prevent-heartburn. Accessed Jan. 1, 2011.

"New Bacteria Strain Points Way toward 'Super Sourdough' Bread." States News Service. COMTEX News Network. HighBeam Research.

"Organic Acids Lower GI of Bread." Emerging Food R&D Report. Food Technology Intelligence. HighBeam Research, 20 Dec. 2010, www.highbeam.com.

Overboe, Annie. "Sourdough Bread Dates to Old West." *Daily Herald* (Arlington Heights, IL), January 17, 2001.

Pitcher, Bill. "Daily Bread of the Colonies." *The Record* (Bergen County, NJ), 2003. HighBeam Research, 20 Dec. 2010, www.highbeam.com.

"Research from V. Giannone and Co-Authors Yields New Data on Life Sciences." *Biotech Week.* NewsRX, 2010. HighBeam Research, 24 Dec. 2010, www.highbeam.com.

"Separating the Whole Grain From the Chaff." Harvard School of Public Health. Nutrition Source website: www.hsph.harvard.edu/nutritionsource/what-should-you-eat/separating-the-whole-grain-from-the-chaff/. Accessed on Jan. 1, 2011.

Sevier, Laura. *Ecologist* 38, no. 2 (Mar. 2008): 52–53.

"Studies from University of Michigan Yield New Information about Allergies." *Biotech Business Week.* NewsRX, 2009. HighBeam Research, 24 Dec. 2010, www.highbeam.com.

Taluja, Tad. *The New York Public Library Book of Popular Americana.* New York: Macmillan, 1994.

Wu, Olivia. "Cook/Chemist Captures Wild Start Bakers Crave." *Chicago Sun-Times*, 1995. HighBeam Research, 21 Dec. 2010, www.highbeam.com.

RECIPE INDEX

CALEB WARNOCK & MELISSA RICHARDSON

CALEB WARNOCK

Caleb Warnock is the author of the national bestseller *The Forgotten Skills of Self-Sufficiency Used by the Mormon Pioneers*. He and his wife, Charmayne, live on the bench of the Wasatch Mountains. Caleb is a full-time journalist and teaches writing in addition to selling pure, non-hybrid seed raised in his own garden and teaching his popular "Forgotten Skills" classes. He can be reached at calebwarnock@yahoo.com. He blogs at CalebWarnock.blogspot.com.

MELISSA RICHARDSON

Melissa Richardson is a mother of three who is addicted to researching, studying, and baking bread. As a college student, Melissa taught herself to bake as a way to pinch pennies from the food budget and unleashed a passion that transformed her into the Bread Geek she is today. At any given time of day, flour can be found somewhere on her shoes, clothes, hands, or children. When not baking or writing, she enjoys collecting hobbies and spending time outdoors with her family. Melissa and her husband, Troy, live in Salt Lake City, Utah, with their three small children.

163

the **FORGOTTEN SKILLS** of
SELF-SUFFICIENCY
used by the
MORMON PIONEERS

CALEB WARNOCK

MANY PEOPLE DREAM OF becoming self-reliant during these times of fluctuating prices and uncertain job security. Using truly simple techniques, you can cultivate the pioneers' independence to provide safety against lost wages, harsh weather, economic recession, and commercial food contamination and shortages. Now you can discover the lost survival skills they knew, used, and passed down for generations—skills such as how to:

GROW HARDY, PERENNIAL, AND LONG-KEEPING VEGETABLES

REVIVE THE PIONEER SEED BANK

BAKE WITH PIONEER YEAST

CREATE A STRAW CELLAR

COOK WITH FORGOTTEN RECIPES

AND MORE!

THE ULTIMATE PRACTICAL GUIDE for the pioneer in all of us, this book will strengthen your family's self-reliance. Discover anew the joy of homegrown food, thrift, and self-sufficient living. Order your copy today!

NOW AVAILABLE AT AMAZON.COM, CEDARFORT.COM, BARNES AND NOBLE, AND OTHER FINE STORES.